The Adventures Of A Drug Addict

Table of Contents

MARCH 22 4
The Turn Out 8
   The Transition 12
The Night Life 16
   The Spot 20
Dysfunctional Players & Vengeful Zombies 23
   SPACESHIPS & ANGELS 29
Pimp Graduation (The BLACK HOLE) 36
   Spiritual Decline 41
Celebrated Chaos & The Fools Theory 46
   The Homeless Scientist 50
The Elevator UP 53
   The ANGEL'S Hand 59
The 5th FLOOR 62
   Getting MARRIED 66
THE HOSPITAL 70
   THE INSANE ASYLUM 72
Looking For A Change 76
   HER NAME WAS ADDICTION 78
THE NIGHT BEFORE 81

The Adventures Of A Drug Addict

Table of Contents

- Our First Date 83
- **SUPPORTING MY HABIT** 85
  - POLICE ROBBERY 87
- **ME & My GIRLFRIEND** 92
  - SUICIDAL RICH MAN 95
- # DRINKING DRIVING ROLLING 101
  - The 5 Year Old Prostitute/SERIAL KILLER 105
- The Resurrection of HATE 108
  - RISE OF A PIMP 110
- 5-STAR DINNING 116
- ## JOE THE DIAMOND JEWELER 120
- **SECRET SOCIETY: THE SET UP** 122
  - Mr. Mystery & Ms. Babylon 126
- # Warrants, Jails, Mama & Bail 129
  - **Famous Clientele** 132
- **THE GLOOM OF ADDICTION** 134
  - The Fall of An ADDICT 136
- **IN HEAVEN DANCING WITH DARKNESS** 139
  - CLUB HEAVEN 142
- # LIVING AS A FIEND 150

Table of Contents

- HARRY: HEIR TO THE THRONE ... 157
- The AFTER LIFE ... 161
  - PLEASE DO NOT KILL ME ... 168
- The Beggar & Levitating ARTIST ... 172
  - FOLLOW THE LIGHTS ... 177

The Adventures Of A Drug Addict

The day is March 22! I am having an argument with the woman who was my common law companion and the mother of my children. It was about her having card parties at our house with a crowd that was not good for a young family. She had also begun hanging out until late into the night, with little regard for our three children who were all under the age of 5. I went to my parent's house to ease the stress. The next morning I returned to locked doors! But I could hear motion from within! The movements coming from the small frame house were too hard to be that of the kids. I looked through the living room window and saw the little ones playing carefree.

I had been thinking; shit had seemed strange and strained for the last few weeks. I could still feel the nervous and negative energy coming from inside of my house. I started to the backdoor! But first I blocked the front door with my car. The back entrance was locked as well.

I remembered a window in the bedroom being unlocked from a few nights before. I had opened it for air during a discussion and argument on being with the wrong people and staying out late into the night. I gently pushed it up. As I was climbing in; someone ran through the hall and dashed out of the backdoor. He was gone. So she would have to endure the wrath of my fury!

I screamed, **"How could you do this to our family?"** I grabbed her and she was floated across the room. I was angry and emotionally fueled. Her head hit the table and then her neck bent awkwardly. I thought it was broke! I ran over to help her and realized that she was fine. I left before I reacted again.

My young son was the youngest at only

sixteen months old. My daughter was two and our oldest was 5. I felt horrible because they saw it all. I remember thinking, **"What a fine example this is for the kids."** I stayed in Louisiana another week; and with much regret, deep anguish and inflated sorrow, I made the choice to leave my beautiful children behind!

I moved to Texas and immediately landed a job with a marketing company. I was fortunate enough to stay with a high school classmate. He was what one would call uptight. And even though I was not any trouble; he did not approve of my marijuana habit or my association with his wild cousin. They had competed with each other throughout childhood and shared contempt for each other. And after four weeks; he politely wrote me a note one day asking me to leave.

My own cousin and I were to move into an apartment together, but he backed out because his girlfriend would be coming soon to be with him. She was a known whore and I considered this to be an act of treachery from someone I was so close to. I warned him that it was a bad idea, and in time, she would leave him for another woman. So, I resulted to the alternative, which was living in my car and cheap hotels to survive this beginning crucial time in the big city of Dallas.

I eventually recovered and landed a gig making $22,000 a year working for a financial institution. This was a huge blessing for me because I was coming from North Louisiana, making less than $8000 annually as a pizza delivery driver. I enjoyed overtime whenever the opportunity presented itself and I developed an even stronger love for money and business.

I was able to move out of the car and into

The Adventures Of A Drug Addict

an apartment. I felt as if I was really becoming a man. I could pay all of my bills. I took care of my own affairs and even saved some money. I was living in the suburbs of Dallas. I had yet to really experience the city life!

At my previous and first job upon arrival in Texas; I met a woman named Renita. She was my manager at the time and we started dating for a while. I even brought her home to meet my family. But it did not last. She was older, moved faster, possessed greater financial stability than me and she was in pursuit of something I would not offer at the time; LOVE. I rejected it from her on the basis of my past. She did however take me downtown to a place where I eventually met a woman named Asia.

She was beautiful. Her skin radiated as the shine of the sun. She had curly locks of old that reminded one of the portraits of the past. She was a writer, an artist and one who was seeking ***"Spiritual Truths."***

We started seeing each other and I fell madly in love with the gentleness of her spirit. She lived about an hour away from me, so I was hardly ever home. Everything was great for about three months but then it became rocky. We started seeing less of each other because she would take frequent trips out of town and I would not hear from her until her return. I thought this was a sign and I began to take it personally.

We broke up but then reconciled. It was during this intermediate period that I landed a job in the accountant department of a local paper. I was making more money than before. We started off strong again. But my trust issues were mingled with great suspicion concerning her trips without me. What I did not know was too much for my heart. My relationship was taking a toll on my work ethic and I eventually was fired from a pleasant situation. We ended for good in June of 2001 and it left me devastated. I heard later that she had moved to be with her child's father. She had told me he was mentally and physically abusive and treated her horribly!

I felt betrayed once more by a woman I felt I had treated with love, respect and loyalty. I danced in my own depression and self-loathing. This seemed to only intensify my pain because I still had not healed from the sudden separation from my children and family a year before.

These thoughts led me to constant drinking in bars and night clubs. This was only a shadow of what was to come. The cup I held in my hand was "*bitter*" and "*full of poisons!*" BUT I CONTINUED TO POUR UP.

The Adventures Of A Drug Addict

Chapter: 2
THE TURN-OUT
(His Anger and Resentment)

I was in the club! My last five dollars was spent on a shot of gin and juice that was floating inside of my bloodstream. It was a pointless beverage because it wasn't enough to ease my pain. As I sat in the cocoon of my resentment and pain, I noticed an attractive young lady of a mixed race with a wild and eccentric blonde hair-do to match. She was watching me with intent. And as I was leaving, she steadfastly crossed my path and came to an abrupt stop! She asked, "What's your name?" I told her and followed by asking hers. "*Suni*, but my real name is Crystal."

She asked me, "Why are you by yourself?" I responded, "It's a lonely world and I am one in it." I asked her the same question and she told me that she was meeting someone for business, but they did not show up. Out of pure curiosity; I asked her, "What kind of work do you do, since it brought you to the club to conduct business?"

She answered, "*I'm a whore*." I said, "**What!**" She boldly restated, "*I'm a prostitute*, and I am here to spread the gospel to the streets." Shock and awe was the expression of both my face and my spirit. She asked me to walk her to her car and I obliged. We continued the conversation as we made our way through the fog of the club.

We arrived at her SUV, which was parked quite a distance from the other vehicles. She gave me her number and asked me to call the following day. Most people would have run and forgot about the whole meeting. ***Not me!***

I looked forward to the next conversation. I made it home and told my friend M.L. about the strange girl. After some reflection I went to sleep.

I called her the next day and we talked for several hours before she asked me to come over for a smoke session. I arrived to the strong scent of weed. She explained that her bud was the best and most expensive. She spent around six hundred dollars a week on her marijuana habit.

Her home was elegant and well furnished. We got high and talked! I spent the night and went home. She called me early the next day. She asked would I come over at 7pm and I agreed. As soon as I arrived she asked if I would be her pimp. My broken heart, plus the pain, anger, fear and resentment encouraged me to say yes.

She left the house and said she would return when she had some money for her new man. I stayed behind, at her house, with her two young boys, ages 10 and 2. They were both from previous relationships with pimps. *It was immediately that my ego took over.* I departed on the road to self-confusion, which was near self-destruction, and so far from the path of truth and self-realization.

She called me on my cell phone every hour to tell me her location. I was very nervous. Every thought included the police breaking through the door to arrest me for agreeing to her request to use her and to help enable her unconventional occupation. My mind dwelled on the fact that I had seen strong and respectable women in my own family. This was so opposite from the way my parents had raised me.

I smoked more weed to ease my mind from the thoughts of truth. I fell asleep on the

The Adventures Of A Drug Addict

couch and awoke to a knock around six in the morning. I anxiously arose to my feet and looked through the peep hole.

It was her! She came in and kissed me on my cheek. She handed me a thousand dollars and said, "*It ain't no money like ho money! I am giving you a million dollar education for free.*" I looked at her with the eyes of a confident, self-centered and egotistical fool. I felt like I was possessed with power. But I was unsure of this situation; and even more than that, I was unsure of myself.

I left her house around ten that morning. I made it to my apartment and told my friend about the night and the new job I had just taken; as a prostitute's manager and pimp. As she slept during the day I went to shop for new clothes. I covered up my soul's feeling of wrong with shopping.

I called her around six and made it to her house at seven that evening. She immediately left for work as a call girl. I watched the kids and talked to her all night, especially during the period in between customers. She made it in at seven that morning.

The money she handed me was six hundred dollars. It was less than the night before, but still more money than I could make in a week at a job. This was the kind of thinking that I used to reprogram myself to deny the spirit within. I handed her back a one hundred dollar bill for food, gas and weed. I then proceeded to my apartment almost $2,000 richer than two days before.

The feeling was spectacular! My eyes had a twinkle that only the negativity of street cash can produce. I was new to the evils of pimping and prostitution, so I kept the money she gave me in my wallet. She recognized it as a sign of weakness and inexperience. She expressed her concerns when she called me later that day. Sunday was off day for prostitutes and pimps; another unwritten rule.

    I went over to her house and got high. She educated me on the rules of being a pimp and about her spirituality. I thought this was odd since she had chosen such an insane way to acquire financial access. She told me her income was anywhere from $12 to $20k a month. It all depended upon her persistence.

    She talked about her younger brother Chicago, who was an up and coming pimp in the streets of Dallas. She thought that I should hang with him for the lessons in which he could teach me about the sins of the sex business. She said we would be introduced upon him coming home from Jupiter Island. I wanted to know why he was in Florida. She said that he sent his whore there two months ago to get some "respectable money;" the kind that she says a pimp can be proud of. He went to pick her up from assignment.

    The next day was Monday and very slow. She only made a few hundred dollars. Her $800 car note, $300 car insurance and $1600 rent was due. I paid it with no problem. I had acquired close to four thousand dollars during my first week in the life. **_Pimping was my new job, recreation, ambition and also my eventual downfall!_**

The Adventures Of A Drug Addict

Chapter: 3
THE TRANSITION

I had sold weed off and on since I was 16. I understood something about the capitalistic, buy/sell mentality of people. It was something that could not be taught in my high school. Those many realities can't be fully distributed nor understood by those who have never lived it. And the terminology used to express such moments in life are unique to the self-condemned and the self-proclaimed hopeless!

It was our third week together and I was going out every night partying, drinking and spending. *It was all on me. I had the tab. I was increasing my appetite for liquor. I had become an alcoholic.*

She would call all night long. I didn't answer because I was swimming in the self-denial of what I was becoming. **I had money, alcohol and my choice of women.**

One night Crystal became upset. She had called and I didn't answer nor call back until hours later. She said a **"trick"** could have hurt her or robbed her of **my cash**. She told me I wasn't up for this job and she would not be my whore any more.

I pleaded for her to come over later that day so we could talk. She came over and we smoked a blunt of the high grade. I locked the doors so that we could have some private time and I could plead my case. Over two hours had passed and she said that it was time for her to go. And as she was about to leave, my cousin knocked at the door.

He had been a best friend since first grade and was now my roommate. His previous girlfriend had left him for her new found lesbian life. During his time of healing from that heartbreak, he had become engaged to another high school girlfriend.

I unlocked the dead-bolt and walked her to her vehicle. When I returned to my domain; my friend immediately confronted me on my visitor. He was ready to preach to me.
Our other friend M.L., who was also staying with us, had told him about this girl and her occupation.

He said, **"Man, you are wrong! What if your family knew about this?"** He said he didn't want a prostitute in the house where he lived. His brother, M.L. and another friend D-town had just arrived as he got deep into his sermon.

They listened to my justifications and his complaints for over two hours. Our lease was close to expiration and he said he was going to live with his now pregnant fiancé. He and I had moved to the city in hopes of having a life in the music industry together, but all hopes of that dual realization shattered with his marriage.

My friend, M.L. was my road dog. He found this new lifestyle interesting and motivating. We talked much about the details.

Crystal had decided I needed to learn more about the role of a savvy and stern pimp, and all of his dictator characteristics. She wouldn't trust me with the income from her sex business until I learned more discipline. I attempted everything except violence to stay in control. It all failed.

I spent most of the money I had on clubs

The Adventures Of A Drug Addict

and drinks. Yes, I spent thousands on going out to be entertained in just a few short weeks. The money went as fast as it came. I spent money on strangers and gave them my time during this initial period of *"mind reconstructing"* and *"soul depreciation."*

    M.L. and I decided to go to a strip club and recruit possible girls. The plan was to teach what I had learned. He found two who were willing. They came home with us after their all night shift of dancing and being *"sexually molested"* by sex crazed men for dollar bills. The guys throw them on the floor for them to pick up like dogs trying to get scraps!

    We explained the teachings with seminar style lessons. One left the next day to go back to dancing for dollar bills. The other would stay for 9 days. Her stage name was Chocolate. She was 19 and still in high school. She worked as a dancer in a low tier strip club. We bought her liquor, weed, clothes and nails for her to embark upon the transition *"from low class stripper to high class escort."*

    We dropped her off at the Adams hotel because Crystal had told me about its upscale patrons. I gave her instructions and told her to go to the bar, order a drink, tip the bartender a twenty dollar bill and tell him that you are bored. He would then point the way to which ever men were in need of female company, and who did not mind spending money on such vices.

    We were hoping she could find a million dollar client like Crystals *"trick"*, who went by the name *"Dick."* Mr. Dick was a CFO for a major corporation based in Dallas. He was a *"by any and all means necessary"* man of ambitions.

These were the most common men seen by the escorts.

They were usually white, middle aged, conservative and ultra-religious married men. They hid their secrets of sexual deviances from their wives, children and the general public.

Mr. Dick was one of them. He had gotten rich by taking the quarterly earnings of the company he worked for. He would deposit these millions of dollars into accelerated interest bearing accounts in foreign lands. These transactions would draw high returns.

He would then leave the money there for a certain amount of time, take the interest, which was usually tens of thousands and finally return the companies money before any overheads or honest secretaries ever knew it was ever gone.

She did not find another Dick, but she did meet two young engineers who paid her $300 to perform oral crimes on them both. She called my cell phone and told us to come pick her up. She got in the car full of excitement and handed M.L. the $300. She said it only took her fifteen minutes to get the dirty and sinful money.

The turn-out had happened. The twinkle had entered her eyes and she was now possessed with the **"demon of street ambitions."** She stayed for another week and then left. It was enough time to push this energy of negativity even further into her being. It would be three years before I saw her again.

GOD, Forgive me!

The Adventures Of A Drug Addict

Chapter: 4
THE NIGHT LIFE
His Inconsiderate Greed & Lust

My roommate had moved in with his pregnant fiancé. She lived in a town about an hour away. M.L had moved back to Louisiana and I was alone and nearly broke. I only had four hundred dollars and days before the lease expired.

The week before, Crystal had introduced me to her brother Chicago. One day she called and arranged the meeting for us. It was scheduled for the weekend. M.L. and I had met him at a strip club, which was far more lavish than the ones we had been to before. The customers were aged, rich and in search of a woman, with whom they could explore their sexual deviances with outside of their wives.

He had on an *"Armani purple suit with Gators to match."* We all introduced ourselves and he ordered alcohol for us. He did not drink nor do any drugs, because he said that was the sure path to insanity in this *industry of tricks, johns, prostitutes, pimps, police, high stakes and evil money.*

He discussed the fundamentals of pimping all night long. He was convinced that this was the best way to achieve maximum financial benefits with no negative consequence to self. He paid the way! Hundreds of dollars were spent between numerous adult establishments that first night and they were all polluted with lost souls seeking the next indulgence of the senses.

We went back to his town home. They were appropriately called the mansions. He stayed in this $2000 a month rental property. His pad was bigger than my working class parent's home. It was equipped with modern furniture. Versace and Armani lay on the sofa like t-shirts that one might work in.

It was eight in the morning before we left. Crystal called to ask how everything went. I said, "Ok."

I was being pulled deeper into the depths of a criminal life, a personal spiritual hell and intense mental illness. The man that my mother and father knew was now dead and a **"heartless pimp was birthed"** in his place. It would be seven years before I would be redeemed, resurrected and reborn in the truth, as *a "Spirit Son of GOD!"*

Crystal was excited about my meeting with her brother and the possibility of him teaching me how to rule her with an iron hand. She subsequently transported close to another two thousand dollars into my hands after I met her brother. I used the money to move into an upscale apartment complex in the north. *There I was! Living on the edge; domiciled on a street called the horizons.*

In my warped and polluted mind; I thought this form of materialistic thinking was worthy. I became even more wrapped up in myself and this twisted way of being. *"That I was" was "That I had become."* I decided I would not work for eleven or twelve dollars an hour, toiling and slaving for wages that couldn't provide adequate security for me and my new lifestyle.

The Adventures Of A Drug Addict

This poor *"Quality of Thought"* would stay with me for years after and affect my ability to stay employed. I figured that my destiny was written in stone and I was determined to follow this sick path to fortune. I knew it was all wrong and much bad would come as a reaction to *"my choice"* to entertain such obvious evil.

I was denying the existence of *"Truth."* But even in this great state of insecurity; I felt the *"love"* of the spiritual forces of the universe still around me, protecting me and not giving up on me. I gave thanks to *"The MOST HIGH,"* even then!

My introduction to the night life was mesmerizing to the *"immature mind"* of my *"pained personality."* We would start our night around 10pm. We were constantly on the prowl for a *"victim"* of their circumstances. *We were the predators of the night.*

We went to club after club. The valet, the doorman and the waitress were all tipped twenty dollars. This type of exchange went on all night; from establishment to establishment. Hundreds of dollars were spent every night in the final attempt to seduce. It was all about the money! Or was it?

In return for the love of money; the service was extra-ordinary! They would tell us about the girls who were more willing than others. They were accessories to the whole operation. The club workers donated to this evil too. It was a full circle of wrong. They were all criminals indeed.

They all gave life to ***"Sin City;"*** the club owner, the ever deceitful patron, the bartender, the waitress, the valet, the security and even the girls. They were the most lost, vulnerable and crooked. I lounged in VIP seclusion with athletes, other pimps, prostitutes, high stakes dealers of narcotics and corporate money men. They ran the underground because they were the main driven force behind ***"Supply and Demand."***

The Adventures Of A Drug Addict

THE SPOT

On one particular night, after most of the clubs had closed around four in the morning; Chicago said, *"I think you are cool. I am going to take you to the spot."* So we got in the car and headed for the west side of town.

We arrived at this worn out and unattractive building with a big steel door. He knocked and a small slide screen opened about the size of a book mark. A man's eyes appeared through the opening?

He looked and said, *"That's you Chicago?"* Chicago answered back, *"yeah."* I heard maybe six locks as they were unsecured. The heavy door to this bubble was opened. We floated in baby.

There was food cooking and it was laid out in buffet style. I saw $300 bottles of champagne on the table. There was beer and ever kind of liquor that was drinkable. The strong drink was needed to persuade this illusive lifestyle of *"spiritual and mental violence"* against the self and others.

I saw multiple pimps in thousand dollar suits and alligator shoes. They all had more than one *"working girl"* on their shoulder and every move. There were dealers with expensive jewelry, braids and white t-shirts.

A dice game was going on at a table in the corner of the room between about ten guys. The amount of money I heard someone yell out as the bet on the table was unbelievable. It shocked me!

A younger fellow in his early twenties said, **"Bet the $19g"!** I saw thirty eight thousand dollars on a bet between these two high rollers. There were other bets being placed but I only focused in on the main one. This older pimp in his fifties had the squares of chance in his hand.

He rolled the dice! Everyone was in suspense as they moved and landed on their choice of dots and imaginary numbers. He crapped out! He paused for a few seconds and so did everyone else.

He said, **"Damn"** and reached down by his ankle. I thought he was going for his pistol to take his money back. Instead his hand reemerged from below the table with two gigantic rolls of money; secured with *"heavy duty rubber-bands."*

He threw the dice to the next man and said, **"Bet the same thing."** It was amazing to my now *"blind eyes."* There had to have been close to a hundred thousand dollars on the table during my ten minutes as a spectator to this defining game of chance; as it concerned them and me.

I thought about guys I knew back home. They would have robbed every man and woman in the room that night. I was only concerned with; how and where did they acquire this money? It allowed them to leisurely bet the amount of a car with a three second roll of the dice.

I was introduced to this **"Pimp named Neptune."** He was Crystal's last dictator and she had told me about him. He was in his mid-thirties. He had the talk and look of an

The Adventures Of A Drug Addict

experienced *"predator"* and he drove a Rolls Royce. He owned two houses in the metropolitan area and one on the west coast where he also conducted business.

He had gotten rich by the sweat, degradation, and sexual exploitation of chiefly one woman over a fifteen year period. She was now in her 40's and looking aged from this vampire type of lifestyle. Neither she nor he was ready to give it up. *"It was all for the love of money or was it"*? He gave me his number and told me to call him. Our night ended. That was the final call of seduction! The money, the false sense of respect, the negative prestige and the fast pace of the streets had completely taken me by both, my own *"choice"* and *"surprise."* It was enough to keep me addicted to the devastating and **"spiritually dead lifestyle"**.

I felt important. I was feeding my ego lies. I was giving my soul the marks of the **"beast"** and he was living inside of me. This potential energy of destruction had been lying dormant until its activation. The fear, regret, anger, resentment and pain were to blame. I used my creative forces for absolute wrong. This path would eventually lead me to **"Heaven"** and the *"After-Life."*

Chapter: 5
DYSFUNCTIONAL PLAYERS
and
The Vengeful Zombies

I observed *"childhood tragedies"* in nearly all of the players. Their past lives were filled with stormy and shady events. They all had issues that could and should probably be diagnosed. Unresolved emotional catastrophes were our disease! Crystal and her brother came from a dark and turbulent past that dictated their philosophy and ideology.

One night, Chicago and I decided to hit the *"Billion Dollar Saloon Club."* We had gone to meet a pimp friend of his who was in town from Canada. He was scouting a new city to bring his five prostitutes to. I was drinking my usual indulgence in a glass; gin and juice plus a chaser of beer. I took a sip of *the "demonic spirit"* and immediately my heart skipped several beats. It then proceeded to rapidly increase to almost five hundred thumps every minute. This had happened before, but not like this.

I walked outside and jumped in my car. I sunk into the seat. *Everything became dark and I blacked out*. I started the journey inside of my body. I thought I was going to die!

I saw the entire world as a reflection of scenes from my life. It was the biggest and most spectacular movie screen ever and it

The Adventures Of A Drug Addict

consumed every space in the sight of my vision.

I saw my birth and my parents. I felt their love during this time as it was coming from behind the display of my life. I saw my own children and relived the joy that they brought to my life.

I recalled my earliest memory, which was one of compassion. I was seven months old and playing with my brother's shoe in my stroller. He cried out in a sad voice for me to return it and I felt sad for him. I restored the object to his hands and he smiled. One of my first thoughts was of quality.

Then, my first sexual memory flashed across the gigantic screen that surrounded me. An older female, who was maybe around twelve, had taught me oral sex. I became both the performed on and the performer. I think this is the beginning of the pain and the resentment I felt towards women.

She would teach me how to make the female wet through sexual stimulation. She held my head and guided me step by step. This occurred around age three or four and it happened several times. I don't fault her for the encounter because it had to be taught to her. So the abuse was a domino effect. I just happened to be one of the dominoes on the table of human events.

Then I recalled being awoke to screams and going back to sleep. I must have been about five. The next morning I was shocked to learn that the kids across the street had lost their mother to the anger and drunken rage of their father. He stabbed her to death. There were frequent police visits to stop the violence. On this one particular night it ended in physical death!

I then reminisced on the single *"most painful event of my life."* My best friend was shot dead, less than fifteen feet from my eyes! A self-inflicted gunshot wound to the head was his way out and his final emotional expression on this earth. *It was a suicide!*

He told me what he would do and I did not take him serious. I drove him to his death! He was sad over the girl he was seeing and her promiscuity. I had been seeing her before hime and so had many others. I knew and he knew she was no good for him. My friend was caring, sincere, loyal and tough all at the same time. He put my first tattoo on my arm.

He told me, that he had found out about her being with this twenty-four year old Man and barber. He liked to target the girls at the high school and Jr. High with his painted car, expensive rims and loud radio.

He wanted to kill both of them, but he could only locate one. The day before, he had put his gun to her head and told her, *"I would kill you, but I only have one bullet and I need three!"*

He said one was for her, the other for the older guy who was taking advantage of her young teenage mind and my friend himself. He had told me that day what he wanted to do but I didn't believe him. It was a boy crying out for help to his best friend. His best friend failed him and it cost the boy his life!

I should have sought help from someone but I did not. That was a choice, in which I have come to greatly regret daily! He shot her and turned the gun on himself the next day. I begged him to put the weapon up and get back into the

The Adventures Of A Drug Addict

car, but he did not!

He looked at me as he made the decision to die. I heard him whisper the phrase of no return as me and another witness pleaded for him to not do it! His last words were, *"Naw G, I'm going to buck this ho!"* Time came to a standstill and the shots ranged out!

From somewhere in Eternity; a powerful voice spoke and said, *"It is nothing that you can do now."* I was left to witness the total collapse of the mind. It was then that I saw the portals of death open above my head and his soul ascended to the unknown!

I could not save him! She survived and I am sure she has suffered greatly from the attempted murder. She was lost and taken advantage of by men then and very little of it was her fault. We were all kids. Maybe she was abused as a child. Everything leads me to believe that this is just the case in her life as well.

That affected me very much; perhaps more than anything else! How does one heal from such guilt, self-blame and shame? How does a kid move pass his past? No one had the answers to my questions.

That was the starting point that my life began to spiral downhill. I began my life of crime soon after. I became involved in extremely risky behavior. A Great Depression ensued!

I sold marijuana at the school and developed a way for me and my friend to get money from the tickets sold at the games! We also were into shoplifting. We were able to get our hands on thousands of dollars' worth of electronics, games and designer clothing. We were in the 10th grade and had access to more money than our teachers. Some weeks I had over a thousand dollars. I somehow managed to barely graduate and went to college.

I had two daughters by two women. The sisters are less than eight months apart. I quit college and moved back home to be with one of my newborn daughters. My son came soon after. I had a family life.

I only wanted to raise my children and be a father at that 19. But that great reality of being a 24/7 dad was shattered by the sight of her having sexual relations in our house. It was the next door neighbor and just too much for my heart. I moved to Texas after learning of her truth and excepting the reality of it all.

It seemed to me, that a woman had been responsible for all of the negativity in and around my life. *I was fed up and started building hate and resentment up towards those I blamed!* I was still seeing my life just like a movie in an I-Max theater.

Then I witnessed me falling in love with *"Asia."* I saw how my spirits were lifted when I met her but then brought back down low by her ultimate absence from my life. I loved her or at least I thought I did. But she just vanished from life and I resented the woman for that. I never heard from her again. It seemed my life was a failure. I did not care if I died, but I did care how my death would affect my family if my death occurred here.

I saw my kids and how they are destined to grow in the love of **"GOD."** I could play a role in this, but only if I lived. I did not want them to have to grow up with the same issues as myself. The vision of them made my soul giggle. I began to think of the future.

The Adventures Of A Drug Addict

Time still had not become a reality.

But then I saw a ***"Black Hole"*** and it started pulling the light from my body. It was absorbing the memories that I had just seen into its vortex. I then saw and felt a great flash of light. It was the most powerful, yet soothing light to ever touch my being. It blinded me and suddenly the vision was over and time began to move again. It took me a few seconds to re-achieve my breathing! I wasted a half-full drink on my pants as I struggled to control the air passage.

I gathered enough energy to walk back into the club and get my associate. He rushed me to the emergency room. I lay in the hospital praying that ***"GOD"*** would allow these doctors to perform healing to my heart.

I should have prayed for the healing of my broken heart, but I couldn't see at the time because human emotions blinded me. The doctors put special medicine inside of my IV and brought this dangerous problem of the heart to regularity. I was free to go, but not before observing the truth; both past, present and future.

This experience slowed down the rapidity of my night time movements for a while. I contemplated much about what I had saw sitting in the car over the next few days. It was enough for me to escape for a moment of reflection, but not enough to secure a change.

Chapter: 6
SPACE-SHIPS & ANGELS

MY ex-roommate and I had once roamed Dallas trying to find fame and money in the music industry. He and another close friend had been to California on an expedition to get signed right out of high school.

They had come within seconds of finding out if they had what it takes to make it in the business. It was during their subsequent return that he and I decided to form a record label in our small home town in Louisiana.

I was only twenty years old at the time of this two year venture to find success in *"rural"* north Louisiana; home to farms, racists, church, guns and the chronic poor. Our label, which included friends from childhood, fell apart when we invested all of our revenues into a local concert. It failed horribly! This was another great factor in my decision to move to the state of Texas.

By this point, I had given up on the whole music possibility, but my ex-roommate had not forsaken the dream of still releasing a platinum *"solo"* hit. He half-heartedly pursued the thought on his spare time, as he was becoming more pre-occupied with the role of the expecting father.

There was a particular studio just minutes away from *"Texas Stadium."* It was housed at the 7th Plaza. We had recorded there several times upon landing in the *"Big D."* One of my cousins, who belonged to a group from back home, had recorded a local hit there. He linked us up with this guy.

The Adventures Of A Drug Addict

It was during this particular night that my ex-roommate had come to stay with me in my new residence. His vehicle needed repair and I stayed close to his place of employment. Plus, his new living quarters, in which he shared with his soon to be wife, was almost an hour and a half from his job. He had scheduled a two hour block to record a hit song at this cave of musical aspirations!

So, around 6pm that hot and sunny August day; we embarked upon a ride in my car and headed to the studio. It had only been days since that *"close to death"* experience at the *"adult establishment"* of *"insane sexual entertainment"* had stimulated my mind to rethink my life.

We arrived at our desired location and my ex-roommate began his artistic endeavors. His session had gone well past the time I expected. I grew anxious in anticipation of my night, since it was only a little after nine. I was ready to head home and get dressed. My new found associate, Chicago had called and was eager to begin the onslaught of fragile persons.

I walked to my vehicle and called Crystal to ease the anxiety. She was just getting into her night as well. She informed me that it was real slow and that she had only made about a $150 thus far. I then seized the pack of cigarettes that caught the attention of my eyes and slid one out of the pack. I put it into my mouth to calm the tenseness of my current immobility. *I lit it!* And with the first inhalation, I was eased with the falsity and poison of nicotine and America's first "cash" crop, tobacco. I gazed into the night sky. It has always been my custom and joy to meditate and think of all of the many undiscovered treasures of living in the vast Universes of Infinite Creation.

I took another pull of the chemical filled stick of disease. I saw the many planes. Some were descending, while others were making their ascent on "**DFW Airport.**" The thousands of lights in the city obscured the beauty of the night sky. The busy-ness of the city was taking away the sight of the stars and planets all together.

I watched the planes for five minutes. I counted twenty-nine during this short segment. It was then I observed a distinct light pass by one of the planes going at a speed I had never witnessed. I knew it was not a meteor because of its close proximity to the plane. I passed it off as just an anomaly. It passed too quickly for me to make a judgment on.

I then saw three more of the same anomalies. They all passed out of my sight within a second, just like the first object. I yelled to Crystal, **"I just saw a UFO or something!"** I became ecstatic! My eyes had never witnessed such obvious sights in the sky.

At that very point; seven more streaked through the sky with the speed of an **"intelligent shooting star."** Then they came back in the same path in which they had come from! I recounted all eleven, but this time they stopped above my radius, as if to say, **"Yes, We see you."** And just as quick; they all continued on their path and were gone from the view of my eyes.

The Adventures Of A Drug Addict

But they were not gone. As if to repeat the dance for my pleasure; one came back and casually flew beside a plane for a few seconds, before speeding ahead and making a perfect sharp right angle turn just feet from the nose of the clunky man-made flying machine. I thought to myself, *"The people aboard that plane had to see that."* And there they were flying in the night like a family of youthful birds. I told Crystal to get out here quick, so that she could also have this fascinating memory to store in her mind for later reference during the long struggle ahead. I kept saying **"WOW"**; over and over again.

She asked if there was anyone else around who could see what I was seeing. It was instantaneous; two men in their late forty's came out of the 7th Plaza, where the studio was housed. I approached them in a very gentle way.

I said to them, **"I see lights flying in the sky and I just want to know if you can see them as well."** One of the gentlemen responded, *"I'm legally blind, I can only see a few inches in front of me!"* His comrade spoke up and said, **"Show me what you are talking about young man."**

I pointed to one of the unidentified objects and said, **"Look, it is right there."** He said, **"I only see a few planes."** The speed of the extra-ordinary flying machine versus the plane confused him.

I then redirected his sight to the correct point of view and observed the excitement in his face as he witnessed, for the first time in his life, the unexplained phenomenon of fast moving vehicles in the night sky. He yelled in intrigue,

"What is that man?" I responded, ***"It must be a sign from the heavens."*** He told me that in all his years of living he had never seen such a sight.

I called my ex-roommate on his cell phone to inform him of the ***"mystical lights"*** in the sky that moved at super speeds. He rushed out! His natural skepticism was no match to the sight of those ***"Star Pilots"*** and the "***crafts***" they glided in.

As he was coming out, a group of fellows who also had a recording studio in the same building had come out for one reason or another. Two of these guys, who was also brothers, would later go on to become ***"Grammy winning producers."*** Another would become a star on the ***"Ricky Smiley Morning Show"*** My ex-roommate came over and said, "What are you talking about?"

I only pointed up! He responded with the same confusion as the man before him and said, ***"What the hell is that?"*** We were all dazed from the lack of information. Everyone was just brain-boggled! He said, ***"Man, I have never saw anything like that."*** The look in my face spoke silent words to him that agreed that I had neither.

The two young producers walked over to find out what the excitement was about. They had two of their acts with them at the time and they all came over to our radius. Before they could get the question out of their mouth; I pointed up and said, ***"Look."***

The Adventures Of A Drug Addict

      Like the others, they fell into the confusion of excitement over the sight of flying objects moving at super-human speeds and gleefully using airplanes as toys. One of the brothers ran and grabbed his camcorder and documented the remaining footage of the night's events. Somewhere there is evidence of this great ordeal on a two-hundred dollar video recorder.

      Crystal made it to the "studio" observatory. She had a chance to step into the realm of the vast unknown. By that time, one of the glowing and revealing conductors from some unrevealed place had come to take a pause directly above us. And there it was! A ***"Brilliant Light"*** had come to give hope to a miniature sample of the *"lost"* population of what seems to be an isolated world; full of the sickness of lacking ***"self-control."*** The craft hovered high above our head, as we viewed its beauty huddled together in a group that had now reached over twenty souls. More had come from the office building that housed the studios. It allowed us to rave at its sight for about one minute and then it shot straight up into the sky. It seemed like it went into space.

      After almost an hour of seeing the ***"flying objects"*** ride beside planes, make zig-zag patterns into the night sky based upon their mood, turn ninety degree, one hundred & eighty degree, three hundred & sixty degree turns and perform disappearing acts that involved flying super speeds until gone from the sight of our earthly eyes; I decided to leave. I gave my ex-roommate the key to my car and I rode with Crystal. We simply drove away. It was quite different from the drivers of the flying ships in the sky. I felt it was a communication just for me. They were saying, "***We are watching you closely. Be careful!***"

The Adventures Of A Drug Addict

Chapter: 7
A PIMP'S GRADUATION
{I See The Black-Hole}

Crystal had not given me any of her prostitution resources in a couple of weeks. Her brother had even encouraged me to dismiss her and find a real whore that I could call my own. *"I took his advice and began my life as a pimp."*

I talked to her on the phone but I paid her no visits. She was about to gain a six-figure sum of cash from a lawsuit. It wasn't in the cards of a predator/pimp to walk away from that type of possibility, but I did!

I was being pulled deeper into this *"bought attention"* and I was growing accustom to it. Chicago and I practically lived together. He wanted me to be his protégé! His BMW was wrecked and he paid me about $800 a week, plus all of the perks that come with hanging with a man who receives over a grand a day from the sweat and deviant behavior of a weakened female. I became the driver that took him to his destinations of darkness.

All of the money which I had acquired was gone. My ex-roommate came over to my apartment one day to ask me if I was interested in selling some weed. He said that we could go half and split the profits down the middle.

It had been almost two years since I had given up the part time job of distributing marijuana for supplemental income. But I needed more cash. So I agreed! He gave me his portion of the needed capital for the initial investment. I made a call and went to pick up a half pound of weed!

I had now become a criminal with two majors; prostitution and marijuana distribution. I began networking. I told the girls at the clubs where we frequented of my product. It took me about a week to gain a few clients and sell out, but it was not enough to sustain my new lifestyle of gluttony and greed. I went back to my supplier to restock on my product. This time I bought two pounds.

I connected with people all over the spectrum of buyers; strippers, pimps, tricks, other dealers of narcotics, patrons at the establishments, wealthy business people and hippie like smokers. **"I was on a roll and in my new role!"** My ego was fueled with false pride and self-centered thoughts. I was feeling real sinister!

The money had started to come in somewhat, but it was still a long way from the type of money Crystal and her pimp brother had introduced me to. Chicago had showed me how he saved his lose coins. He had over two thousand dollars in silver and single one dollar bills stashed away in a used water jug that once supplied countless drinks to some entity's lobby.

I thought that was a good idea and during my first couple of weeks into dealing; I managed to save a few hundred bucks in quarters, nickels and dimes. **"I had leased my soul to the devil"** and I could see me one day living in a mansion and driving a fancy car. I thought about the money I could send back home to my family and the things I could buy.

There was only one problem. I felt alone on my own! I pushed the lingering issue to the

The Adventures Of A Drug Addict

back of my awareness and kept pushing towards the shallow ideals of pimping, prostitution and dealing. No thoughts of getting an education or finding the spirit within; just instant-gratification to seduce my senses and to keep my mind away from the decaying pain felt by my heart!

I still talked to Crystal and she appeared to be eagerly excited about my further descent into the depths of the **"*underworld!*"** Chicago and I were still hanging close. I was something like an assistant; the kind that entertainers have.

He was a pretty generous guy with a bigger than life ego as well. It started to widen the gulf between us. His ego and my ego began to clash. He had more than a tendency to make one feel as if he was king and all others were only glorified servant. I witnessed more of this trait with each passing day. I could not handle nor was I willing to tolerate anymore. That sort of behavior sparked the radical revolutionary inside of my being.

It had been almost three months since I had started to ride with Chicago almost daily. I was beginning to get fed up with his slick and sly demands, which to me appeared as authoritarian. He made me feel as if I was also a victim of his fast talking and money moving ways.

The revolution had begun in my mind. He had met another girl from one of the adult establishment where we recruited. She was a beautiful brunette with the figure of an hour-glass. She drank and put powder up her nose. After her shift was over, she would come over to his house to relax and **"*get injected with the lies of a pimp.*"** Afterwards; she would pass into the dead-like rest of a vampire.

I had observed her routine for close to week and also the money she made nightly. It appeared to always be close to a grand. I decided this was the end of the road for me and my schooling as a pimp. I did not want to be no man's assistant because I thought I could do this evil myself.

Chicago and I went to her place of nude entertainment. It had become our custom since he was recruiting her to come join his *college of sexual exploitation*. She came over after her shift ended at four in the morning; into what she thought was a place of luxury and solace from the men who only enjoyed her for her body. She was tired upon arrival and immediately retired to the bed.

I waited for about an hour and saw the lights to off. I got her keys off of the kitchen table and headed to her car. I opened the door with the quickness of a professional burglar. No time was wasted!

It took less than a minute for me to locate her earnings for the night. I put the cash in my shoe and casually walked back into the house. I laid the keys back on the counter. I knocked on Chicago's door and told him I was leaving. He said he would lock the door. I grabbed my sports jacket, my packages of marijuana and without hesitation; I closed the door to his pad for good. He was no longer a reality to my being and I had made sure by my action. I got into my car and left.

I had plotted and stolen from a woman who was already getting her youth robbed and extorted from daily. I paid those thoughts no attention and justified my actions by her way of

The Adventures Of A Drug Addict

living. I made the thirty-five minute ascent to my apartment on the Horizons.

I arrived at my living space and parked the car. I ran upstairs and took a shower. It was hard to wash this shady episode from my brain. I broke up the sticky green substance and put it inside of a gutted cigar. Now came the *"insane fun"* part of the day; counting the money I had taken from a young woman; who had taken it from the tricks at the strip club. We were all *"lost"* and *"turned-out."* I counted eight hundred and thirty-seven dollars.

My evil was fulfilled and I felt no regrets at the time. If I could go back; I would team up with what is right and try to guide her to a place of peace, but I was lost too. I pray she made it out of the ills of the night-life.

I knew my association with Chicago had come to an end with that decision, but I was ok with it. I had graduated myself from the class of pimping prostitutes or better yet, preying on weak victims who were victims of their own circumstances. After receiving my degree in this shady business; I embarked upon my own journey to make a name for myself as a *"pimp!"*

Chapter 8
SPIRITUAL DECLICE

I was now ready to fall into even greater levels of insanity and declination. I had come to define my life as being in clubs and entertaining strangers for the pleasure of a dollar. This was done with the realization that eventual trouble would ensue. It was only a matter of time!

I had befriended three ladies who wore different scarves to represent their lives. They all had honest jobs, but all came from troubled settings. I began to distance myself from the adult establishments of nudity and I focused in on the marijuana distribution operation that I had put together. The customer base had increased to the point of a thousand dollars a week.

Her name was Tatiana. She was from the islands and I met her at the same location as I had met Crystal. It was her birthday and as I was leaving she stopped me to inquire about my phone number and to flirt. I told her of my weed operation and she informed me that she was a habitual smoker.

She worked as a loan officer and had a seven year old daughter. She would come by my apartment several times a week to buy and talk to me about her many issues. I listened! We became closer after I became very sick and she gladly took me to the hospital because I was too weak to drive.

She propositioned me to allow her to help me sell my product. I agreed to give her a thirty percent commission on all distribution that came through her. The business grew! She swiftly

The Adventures Of A Drug Addict

began to become subservient to my words and my behaviors.

Then there was Sarah. She was also a young single mother. She was from my home state of Louisiana and too had come from a past of abuse and emotional anguish. She was sweet and had a youthful kindness about herself. I met her at a pawnshop. One of the buyers had given me gold in exchange for the smoke he wanted from me. I had taken it to a pawnshop on the north side of town and saw her there seeking cash to pay a bill.

I asked her for her name and her phone number. Tatiana had helped me to increase my revenues by almost five hundred dollars a week and Sarah looked like someone who could also push me to my goal of two grand a week. I called her and inquired about her financial stability. She told me that her job as a security guard wasn't meeting the demands of her and the one year old daughter she had acquired with her babies daddy, who was now incarcerated for armed robbery.

I told her of my business and she connected me with a guy who offered me better wholesale deals on the weed by the pound. I gave her the same contract as Tatiana; a thirty percent cut on all products that she sold.

I had started to make enough to spend my days in the department stores and malls due to my augmented income. One day while on a shopping experiment at the highly materialistic galleria; I met Maria. She was taking a smoke break from her job as a massage therapist to the pre-Madonna and pretentious upper-class of North Texas. I approached her because she looked like an artist. She gave me her name and contact information, so I called.

She also was the single mother of a six year old daughter. Her child's father had become a crack addict somewhere in the toddler years of their daughter's life. She was a musician and a very free spirit.

She was a decent person with a youthful innocence. I wanted to just be friends with her but she wanted more. We began to hang together in local clubs that allowed our commonality in music to be nourished.

She quickly noticed my fast paced lifestyle. One weekend I asked her if she wanted to go to Houston with me to visit a friend. It was during this trip that she helped me to reestablish my commitment to being a full blown street hustler.

On the drive back, she asked me **"Can I work for you?"** It took me by surprise because I had never approached her with any instigation to sway her down my path. I said, **"Do you want to help me sell my product?"**

She responded, **"Yes!"** But then went on to say, **"But, I want to be your stripper as well and whatever else you got for me to do."** This took me into even further shock and amazement. I pondered for a few minutes and asked her why.

She said, **"I just want some excitement and I will give me all the money like a good worker is supposed to!"** I did not want to corrupt her because she had become a friend. But she

The Adventures Of A Drug Addict

insisted and I was overtaken by greed and lust. I began to orchestrate another diagram in my head, as to where she could go to work and make the money in which I could spend effortlessly in hours.

I concluded the plan and took her to the **"Adult Establishment of Nudity"** that following Monday. She was excited about the possibility of dancing nude in front of strange men and being desired. We arrived at the chosen environment. It was called the **"Part-Time Gentleman's Club."**

I had reentered the arena of **"Pimping and Prostitution."** She made under a hundred dollars her first night, but that was a hundred dollars I didn't have and she got the encounter that she wanted! **WOW!** This was the **"Poor Quality of thought"** I had come to represent. I was even willing to push or guide loyal associates into dishonest and deceitful endeavors. Nothing mattered but today's money! And she took to her new job as my dancer in another man's atmosphere to heart.

During her second week she made quite a bit more money than the week before. She came to my apartment after her shift every night. She distributed **"One Hundred Percent"** of her earnings to me. She did not have to but she did. **"She worked during the day as a respected massage therapist with healing hands."** But by night, she was the dancer of a self-proclaimed pimp and drug dealer.   I had three women during this time and they were all fighting for my attention. They all were offering me monetary gifts in the form of loyalty and criminal labor. Upon Tatiana learning of Sarah's new line of work; she wanted in. Three days later she joined an adult club. It was called **"Crazy Bitch"** in Spanish.

In less than 6ix months I had managed to reprogram my living to be a *"slave to materialism, selfishness, conceit, egotism, greed, lust, inconsideration, pride, gluttony, alcohol, anger, resentment, denial, self-justification, self-importance, defiance, grandiosity, shame and guilt."* I felt nothing in response to any of those feelings nor did I realize that I had become so entrapped! My heart had become so cold! And my mind had started to plot on and manipulate the people that were in my circle. I gave them revenge for the **"sins of others."** It came in the form of **"insane behaviors."**

I was now traveling **"light-speed"** and going deep into the **"outer-realms of darkness!"** Moving so fast is a lonely experience. I was headed for that black-hole I had seen in my mind's eye months earlier at the "Billion Dollar Saloon" and my gear was set in **"SPIRITUAL DECLINE!"**

The Adventures Of A Drug Addict

Chapter 9
CELEBRATED CHAOS
&
The Fools Theory

I began to marvel at my own ego and soon developed an **"arrogance"** that only a **"fool"** can have. I prided myself on the money and the shallowness of such thoughts.

"Disarray and chaos" had put clothes on and we all danced!

My life seemed great because I had learned to identify with being a fool; and I was living it. Day and night was spent in a non-stop campaign to discover the treasures of the **"Fools Theory"** thinking. By day I occupied my home office and kept in touch with the girls.

I collected revenue and restocked them with more products. I was doing a lot of nothing in terms of self-growth. I had become stagnant; not by the world's standards but by the **"Spirit's standards."**

One of my childhood friends had come to stay with me to escape the monotony and racism of Northern Louisiana. He had the chance to witness the precursor to my life as a **"Drug Addict."** I was falling and falling and falling fast!

Tatiana came over one night to inform me of a repeat customer that was willing to spend over a thousand dollars on **"private dances"** away from the **"Adult Establishment of Nudity."**

I told her to set the occasion for the next day at my apartment. The date was confirmed. Friday it was!

A deposit of six hundred dollars had to be delivered to me upfront as proof of his sincerity. The next day she called me to the club at around Midnight. I casually walked in to check out the *"Trick"* and to *"Check my Money;"* as I had every week on that same day.

She gave a clandestine smile. I went to the corner table in the back and waited on her to give me the signature and contract. Both came in the form of an envelope, stuffed with the agreed upon security bond of six hundred dollars; non-refundable. I put the cash in my suit pocket and headed to the bar to have a drink before heading home to await the arrival of Tatiana and the *"Trick"* who lusted after her.

She left her shift an hour early so that she could come over and rest before having to further entice the man with the "Sexual Perversion. At around 1:30 in the morning I heard a knock. It was not her. It was Maria.

Maria came in and told me it was a good night and handed me five hundred dollars in mostly one dollar bills. She was excited and drunk. I guided her to the sofa and laid her down to counter her potential *"Alcohol Poisoning."*

Just as I laid her down, Tatiana called and said she was at the gate. I opened it and moments later she was at the door. She too was full of the intoxicating liquid.

She came in and handed me a small brown plastic bag that contained her earnings for the night. She also had gotten paid from her day job and gave that to me as well. It was a total of $2500. I went and grabbed a beer out of the

The Adventures Of A Drug Addict

freezer and waited.

Tatiana received a call on her cell phone from the **"Middle Aged Married Man"** that spent his nights in the strip clubs propositioning young women for sexual favors in exchange for his cash. She drove to the gate to meet him. They walked up and into my domain. She led him straight for the spare bedroom.

After about twenty minutes, she started to curse and yell. I went into the room and she told me he tried to hold her down and take off his pants. She started to scream and he covered her mouth with his hand. She was scared, and even though I was in the next room; it still was dangerous for a young lady to be dealing with such shady male characters.

He said, **"Man, is this all I get for my money?"** I told him he had to leave or get hurt and that he would see no return of the money that was agreed upon. I went and **"grabbed my gun"** out of the closet and put it on the table and told him once more to leave. This time he quickly and effortlessly headed for the door, but not before tipping Tatiana another hundred dollars. It was not because he was sorry for his aggression and **"possible rape"** of this woman who told him **"no,"** but because of his habit to frequent the club where she worked.

After his exit from my domain; I went and got all of the money that had come into my possession that night. I took the infected cash from the paper bag and the envelope. I slowly and arrogantly began the addition and multiplication of the money that was before me and the problems I was creating.

I counted $3500. It came to me by ways of tainted hands. The filthiness of man and all of his ***"Animalistic Behaviors"*** were centered and ***"Celebrated Chaotically"*** inside of this money, in which I gazed upon with the intent to worship.

The Adventures Of A Drug Addict

Chapter 10
THE HOMELESS SCIENTIST

It was a Holiday! And on Jan 1, my ego's *"dark spirit"* was in a state of constant intoxication! I had been liberated financially. I had three women who were all madly in love or lust with this *"Conceited Character"* I had created out of *"Anger and Resentment."*

The night before; I celebrated in the privacy of my own pad with Tatiana and Maria. We brought in the New Year in silent fashion. I meditated on the material pleasures that I was receiving. I overindulged in everything from sex to alcohol.

I awoke the next morning by the eagerness to go and shop for sunglasses and hats. I proceeded to a favorite shopping locale to obtain the tint for my eyes. It was not far from my place.

I swiftly arrived and I descended from my car to the pavement and finally to the entrance of the shop. I gazed around for less than five minutes before abruptly selecting two, as it had become my tradition to buy in pairs. I entertained the young *"Arabian Owner"* with worthless chat about the perils of city life before starting the path to retrace my steps back to my *"Road Master."* I had been in the store less than ten minutes!

As I left the entrance; I observed a shirtless homeless man in forty degree weather. His body was in superb shape with a very natural tan. He had an umbrella attached to a cart with a seven ring symbol engraved on its side. The umbrella covered his face from the sun while he lay on the sidewalk. It was shining rather brightly in the spot he had chosen to occupy!

He said, **"My son, can I help you out with some words of truth?"** His question came as a surprise to me. Usually it is the one without home who needs the help!

I stopped and asked him his name. He said, **"Just call me Mista."** I said, **"Mista, what words of truth can a homeless man offer me?"**

He said, **"Son, you have much to learn about the world."** He told me he was given a thousand dollars on Christmas Eve by the goodness of even some of the worst people that the city has to offer just by asking. He said that just a small **"act of kindness"** can open the flood gates to **"better living in life"** and **"better thinking in the mind!"**

He went on to inquire about my occupation in life before stopping my words to tell me that he already knows of my ways. He said, **"Son, you are about to witness a spiritual collapse that will take you years to resolve!"** I was intrigued at this point, but still defiant on receiving his obvious blessings.

The shirtless man went on to tell me that incorrect thinking is what denounces most men to levels of insanity and even homelessness. I said, **"If you know all of this; why**

The Adventures Of A Drug Addict

are you homeless?" He looked at me and smiled! He said, *"I am only homeless at this moment in time, but change can occur at any time that I chose."*

We had talked for close to twenty minutes before he told me that his flight was leaving soon. He told me he wanted to leave me with some advice. He said, *"Always keep your head above water, even in the dark and uncertain situations of life."*

He arose from his spot in the light of the sun and gathered his cart with the seven circles on the side. He bid me farewell with a very sincere handshake and the beautiful spoken words, *"Be blessed!"*

He walked away knowing that I watched him leave. He had to have been someone sent to help me see what I could not see for myself. I could not be intimate with his words at the time of the occurrence because it would have stopped me from the addiction. And I could not let that happen. I had valiantly fought to possess it. The *"Addiction to Drama"* was heavy in my being, because I felt as if I was unworthy to live and love in a healthy way. I dreamed of death!

Chapter 11
The ELEVATOR UP

Tatiana had begun to become easily agitated. She had a very short temper as well as a very aggressive attitude. She suffered from a strained relationship with her mother that took a mental toll on her daily. She also had unresolved issues about her father being absent from her life and she blamed her mom for his nonattendance!

She was an occasional user of the ecstasy pill. I did not think it was a problem since I hardly ever saw her do it. But I suspected she was taking more of them during this time of extreme mental stress.

I started to observe her become energized with explosiveness. She befriended one of the girls at the establishment of nudity where she danced for money. I did not support the use of narcotics at the time because I had seen so many of the dancers walking around as "zombies" fueled with the substance of "whatever!"

Tatiana was exhibiting very impulsive behavior and at times, frightening. I discouraged her from this behavior even though I did nothing to stop her from her career as an "exotic dancer." I began to see that her mind was already fragile from extreme resentment and anger towards her past. She was undergoing a nervous breakdown right before my eyes.

I needed to go back east to visit my family and retrieve my children for the holidays. I had planned to bring them back to the

The Adventures Of A Drug Addict

*"**Metropolis**"* so that we could spend time together; just a father and his kids! I decided to take Tatiana with me so that she could clear her mind.

It was during this trip that something went off the rails in her mind. She told me that seeing me and my family's closeness was too much for her to bear. Not long after those words, I started to witness a person who worried me based upon their unpredictability. She began to scrutinize the least insignificant details with loud aggressive words about nothing. No place was safe from her potential ***"Outburst of Anger and Rage!"***

I decided to cut the three day weekend short because of the potential embarrassment she would bring upon me at some point. I had no idea that she had more to offer in terms of *"Possessiveness and jealously."* The damaged heart is so dangerous! The human mind is so easily swayed to insanity!

It was during our return that I witnessed the depths of what ***"resentment"*** has to offer. The ride back to Texas was one of enduring torture! The music blasted at the highest decimal imaginable! Her face occupied a permanent frown.

My kids were only toddlers at the time. But Tatiana's daughter was seven years old and had to witness her mother's mental decomposition. It was her ***"Cycle."***

The trip came to a halt about twenty-five miles outside of the city when a *"chance"* flat tire occurred on the car. She immediately called her mother, whom she had told me practiced forms of sorcery and witchcraft when she lived on her native island. She yelled over the distorted music, **"Bitch, I know you trying to kill us!"** I was dumbfounded! She went on to say, **"When I get back home I'm going to kill you!"**

She hung up the phone and started a lecture of assaulting words filled with hate! They were all directed at the object of her perceived misery. She told me that she knew her mother was responsible. I was dumbfounded!

I tried to talk some logic into her mind. All attempts failed horribly! I rushed to change the tire because cars were passing along the Interstate 20 corridor at speeds high above the limits. She stood at deaths door on the highway, which was only feet from the lane of traffic and she kept pouring her cup full of more hate for the woman who had birthed her!

I made contact with a successful and quick tire replacement and we were on our way, but it came with a price of more negotiations to steer her clear of her mind's intentions. We made our first stop at her house because my car was parked there. The depth of her mind state had not been revealed in its totality to me.

I assumed it was not as serious as first observed. I would soon learn that was a naive way of seeing the obvious! That thought prompted me to stay at her house for the night since we arrived late. I securely tucked away the children and headed for a battle in the bedroom. I took my clothes off and prepared to pass into some form of rest from the day's long events. Within minutes she started her attack on my being. I decided to sleep on the couch in the living room after a back and forth argument

The Adventures Of A Drug Addict

about her mother.

At three that morning I was awoke by my basic instinct! It told me someone was watching me. My eyes opened with the excitement of a startled new born baby! It was her! She was staring intently over my sleeping body! I thought she had come to apologize via intimacy or to fight.

Either way I dismissed her because I was tired. She had consumed my mental and emotional energy that day and the whole month leading up to this episode. I told her to go back to bed and she started cussing me before retreating to the back. At 3:49 am she returned. I had fallen into a deep sleep. It was the first time during the last two days that I could remember actually being in a state of rest.

My body relayed the message to my brain that ice was on my shirtless chest. My sight focused on the area of the one cold spot that my skinned vessel observed. It was a *"six inch knife"* that had cooled the chest area!

I thought I was dreaming until I went to lay my head back on the pillow. During my head's three inch journey back to the complete comfort of the pillow; I saw a single string of hair blow into my sight. I followed it back to its source. It was her!

I grabbed the knife off of my chest and threw it across the room. My hands went straight for her two wrists. I had to make sure I had protection from the other possibilities. The next thing to happen was her landing on the coffee table.

I ran into her daughter's room to check on the children! They were all right. I exhaled internal relief!

I went back into the room but she had left. I walked to the bedroom and was sneaked attacked with a cordless phone to the head. I had become insecure about this situation because my two young children were in this *"house of hostility, rage, resentment and anger!"*

I had to calm the situation to make a safe escape. I had to get the kids to safety. The second round of hostage negotiations began.

I tried to speak in logic, but that route failed and only enhanced her psychosis. My next approach was via the senses. I began to talk and touch her in ways to stimulate her. It worked.

I told her that the children and I would go get breakfast and afterwards I would take them to a family member's house for a few hours while she and I had some alone time. It was now close to the sunrise and I had not slept in days. Her behavior was so out of control that I perceived a great degree of danger in just leaving with the kids.

She had the look of a *"child playing with a gun."* I could not leave her daughter in the house with this person I did not know. I told her that I would also be taking her with us as well, so my kids would have someone to play with.

It worked and at 6:22am I walked out of the door. I headed to my apartment. We had escaped or at least thought it.

She called by the time I arrived to my domain and restarted the extreme *aggressive verbal abuse*. She said that she knew my plan was to help her mother kidnap her daughter. I

The Adventures Of A Drug Addict

now had come to a realization that I had paid for front row seats to be a witness to mental collapse!

I pleaded with her to gain some sanity but my efforts went unrewarded. The level and intensity of her profane words and the accusations of preposterous crimes against her daughter spoke genuine truth to my heart. She needed immediate help and her daughter was in harm's way living with this person who was a potential danger to self and all others.

I did not want her to bring trouble to the uptight neighborhood I resided in. I bought more time with the promise of coming back over after I took the children to the false destination. I told her I would also purchase the drug of her choice before my arrival. She knew I did not approve of it, but overlooked it because it was what she wanted to hear.

She had called me from her mother's house on several occasions and the phone number was on my Caller ID Box. I called unprepared for what I would soon witness? I reached out to the woman that she loved but also hatefully begrudged!

Chapter 12
THE ANGEL'S HAND

I called Tatiana's mother in hopes of finding relief for her issue and to inform her that I had her grandchild in my care. I was seeking first to provide for the wellbeing of the kid. The response I received from this grandmother was shocking.

She answered the phone. I quickly told her of the events that had occurred since Tatiana had called her after we had the blown tire. I explained to her that she had put a knife to my chest and accused me of being a conspirator with her in a plot to kidnap her daughter. The mom just listened for a few minutes without interruption. Then she spoke!

With a very strong accent from an island nation; she said, ***"How dare you bring this upon my daughter?"*** She went straight forward into cussing and aggression. I was even more confused at this point since I had told her that her grand-daughter was with me because I feared for her safety. None of that mattered! She would not let me get a word in.

The woman I had previously met and who looked like a sweet grandmother was replaced by a hostile woman with a fowl mouth! She spoke harshly about her daughter and said that she was worthless. I soon grew tired of all of the verbal negativity.

I tried to bring the conversation back to the important question at hand! Who would see after this little girl? It was then that she said something that appeared to be more than just words from her mouth!

The Adventures Of A Drug Addict

She spoke, "I will curse your children and I hope that harm finds them today." It was then, as she was speaking these words that my son came into my bedroom and decided to sit on the window's edge. I had opened it for some fresh air to aid in dealing with this hostile and bitter woman. A hundred times that window had been opened and just as many times I had checked the safety locks on the window's screens to verify its security.

Just as he sat down; the window screen came off. My **"Dear Son's"** back proceeded to follow the same passageway. I jumped off the bed to grab him but we had at least four feet between us. My mind went into a one second breakdown. It was then that the **"Apparition of a Single Hand"** reached down from out of the ether and captured his collar. It then yanked him back into the safety of the room.

He fell on the floor and I held my son in my arms. We both looked out of the window and saw the screen still tumbling to the ground from its third story jump! It made its landing after about four seconds. Immediately after finding rest upon the Earth; I looked at my only son and he looked back at me.

He did not have a clue of what had just happened and how he was saved by the **"Hand"** that came from nowhere! I hugged him in my arms as if he had just come back to life. I felt the greatest relief a man could ever feel! I was so scared!

I thought about that experience and the pain I would have had in my being forever if something had happened to my child that day. I replayed it over and over in my mind.

Just the thought maintained a sickening feeling in my stomach and head. I felt guilty. I felt so much remorse and so much insecurity; but at the same time I felt blessed beyond belief over the saving "**Hand**" I had just witnessed and the realization that my son will be alright and protected!

    I remembered the curse of the lady that I was talking to before this incident of awareness. I located my phone off the floor and yelled hello. The sinister voice laughed and said, **"Did he fall far?"** I was astonished! It was as if she had seen everything!

    It felt as if she had manipulated the air to make an unfortunate event transpire! But it couldn't have been. I told her to come and get her grand-daughter without delay and hung up the phone. She arrived an hour later and I walked outside to tell her that I did not want to see her nor her daughter anymore. I thought that was the end of my relationship with Tatiana and her mother, but it wasn't!

    Over the next seven days the situation would come to *"reveal the rehearsal of good versus bad, peace versus chaos and choice versus action!"*

The Adventures Of A Drug Addict

Chapter 13
THE 5th FLOOR

I felt relieved! The *"Hand"* in the window had started a journey of minimum reflection inside of my mind. I sat for the next two hours just enjoying watching the sight of my children at play. The simplicity of their movements and the joy of them just being in the world overpowered my heart to rejoice in tears. I thanked *"GOD"* for them. I also thanked *"GOD"* for saving my son's life. *"HE"* also saved my life that day; as *"HE"* has done so many times before during my life of errors, imperfections and pain.

I was closing in on change and I could feel it. There was no denying the vision or its significant revelation. The *"voice of reason"* was starting to speak in my native language and I began to listen! A small tingle and vibration originated in the region between my eyebrows. But like clock-work, the hands of materialism called to blind me with its shine!

The vibration I felt inside of my forehead was soon replaced by a vibration from the cellular phone attached to my hip. It was Maria! She told me that a friend of hers wanted to spend three hundred dollars on a package of my desired product.

I could not turn down the deal since I had abruptly fired and separated myself from Tatiana; who was bringing several thousand dollars into my oversight every month. I told her to meet me at a drop off location to exchange the cash for the merchandise.

We scheduled to co-ordinate the time with her arrival at her first career later that evening.

I heard a knock at the door as I was speaking to her. I looked out of the peephole. It was Tatiana. She had come by with the rage of a soldier at war. Her eyes were filled with anger and her facial muscles were defined like a body builder. Her body language exuberated impatience.

I warned myself to not answer the door, but I had too. I kept my stash at her house and I needed to retrieve all of my business soon. I opened the door.

She rushed in and grabbed me by my neck, as if to beat me. I recovered quickly and threw her unto the couch. She yelled, **"I'm going to kill you! I'm going to kill you!"** I called her name and told her to calm down but she did not!

We struggled for several minutes. Her strength was extra-ordinary and her resolve was impeccable. Finally she stopped resisting and suddenly the look on her face changed to one of calmness and serenity. My mental bewilderment was overwhelming.

She began to talk as if nothing had happened. Her strength withdrew back into the place it had come from. She now began to talk to me with the voice of a little girl. She called herself Anne. I still thought that maybe she was on drugs and just needed some help for that.

All of a sudden she was being sweet and submissive to my every word. She wanted to please me in any way possible. I told her that I needed to pick up my merchandise from her house. She said that she had brought some of it with her. It was just enough to conduct the deal

The Adventures Of A Drug Addict

that I had with Maria. I took possession of the Marijuana and concocted a story to assure a safe exit.

She agreed to everything! I had never observed her in this state of being. It was surreal! She told me that the rest of it was at her house. I was living between her house, Maria's and my own; so I had my possessions scattered among all three. I informed her that I would come by and pick up some of my things because I was going to the cleaners. She said OK and left. She never asked me about her daughter who had left her sight some hours before.

I went to drop off the package to Maria and took my children on an outing to a pizza restaurant that is known for its games and famous cheese eating rat. They enjoyed themselves but my thoughts were lost in translation.

I wondered out loud, ***"How the Fuck am I going to get myself out of this mess?"*** I left the restaurant and headed over Tatiana's house to recover what was mine and to end our short lived partnership. I arrived; and as I pulled up, I saw familiar items on the ground below her window. She had thrown some things out of her second floor window to the ground. I saw cloths, pictures and small pieces of furniture.

I walked up to the door not knowing what to expect. It was wide open. Her furniture was overturned. Clothes and food from out of the refrigerator littered the floor of her once clean and neat apartment. I thought maybe someone had come and robbed her. I did not know if she was dead or alive.

I had a level of fright running through my veins. I walked in! I didn't see her. I called her name and on the third yell she answered.

She said, *"I'm in the bathroom."* I walked in and saw a horrible sight. She was standing in the mirror with a handful of her own hair in her hand. She looked at me and then *"ripped that chunk of hair out."* She had no scissors or any other instrument to aide in this insane practice.

I watched as she let the hair fall to the ground! It led my attention to the fact that other multiple portions of hair had followed the same path to the cold tile floor. I inhaled! Then as I exhaled; I looked at her again and saw that she had pulled nearly all of her hair out.

My eyes had never witnessed such insanity. The sight of a *"woman"* pulling her own hair from the head was terrifying! She did not hold any deliberation of future insecurity about her latter appearance. Her head was tilted like the Eiffel Tower and she was smiling like a tourists looking at it. But yet her face told the truth; a *"severely mentally ill person."*

She had taken on the role of the girl by the name of *"Anne."* She spoke in a low tone and subdued vocalization. But then someone else arrived and *Anne* became *"the Oracle."*

The Adventures Of A Drug Addict

Chapter 14
LET'S GET MARRIED

    She began by raising her voice to a sharp high pitch. The words out of her mouth were unbelievable. She told me that she knew that I had come over to get my things. I quietly said under my breath, **"Yeah."** That should have been very obvious.

    But she also said that she knew of my meeting with Maria. I said to myself, **"Hmm, so she followed me."** As I was accessing the facts in my head; she told me that she knew how much money the deal was worth and that was why she had brought just that amount earlier in the day!

    I did not know what to think. My head spun out of control! How did she know this? Did she set this up with Maria? Did she have my phone tapped? Each question came back with **"no."**

    I was not afraid but the day's words and sights had worn on me. She had become possessed! This was something more than just coincidence. Who had I got myself involved with?

    I needed to go. But I couldn't leave her in this condition. I decided to call the woman who had just tried to curse me and my kid and also the one who had apparently cursed her own child! She answered the phone and I told her of the chaotic scene and the danger that Tatiana posed to herself and any other unsuspecting stranger! She lived right down the street and said she would leave in five minutes to check on her daughter.

I informed her that I would wait at the gate and leave upon seeing her. She agreed.

I stepped back into the mayhem and informed Tatiana that I was going down the street to get a cold drink and that I would return in less than fifteen minutes. I told her to wait. I gathered my belongings and headed to the car. But I could not find the marijuana! I got in and drove my car to a location of relative camouflage since I did not trust this woman.

I saw her expensive foreign car drive through. There was no need for me to stick around. I calmly headed back to my house.

I started to reminisce about all I had seen on this spring day filled with all kinds of disorder. I got the kids upstairs and prepared to have some quiet time mixed with rest. I thought I was ready to depart from this stage of my life, but wasn't! But just as I started to wind down; Tatiana came by with the fury of a storm.

She beat and banged on my door but I refused to answer. Yelling and wailing was her reality and everyone was part of it. I came out and told her to go away after about five minutes. She took off her jacket and it revealed the **"Pound of Marijuana"** I had left over her house.

She started breaking it apart and throwing it to the ground. She was screaming, **"Come arrest this drug dealing pimp."** I did not know what to do to calm her down. I begged her to come in and after some careful coercion; she did!

I picked up the weed. I needed to make sure that she would not restart her engine; so I asked her to stay for a few hours. I let a few hours pass and said that I wanted to hang out at

The Adventures Of A Drug Addict

her house. I told her I would meet her there in an hour.

She said OK, even though I repeated the same tell several times over the last twenty-four hours. She went and I headed to Maria's house. I camped out with her for the next two days and allowed our children to play together since they were around the same age.

On the third day; the phone ringed. I took a look and it was Tatiana's mother! I had not spoken to Tatiana since the day I had left her in a state of insanity.

I answered because I did want to know if she was alright. Her mother spoke to me very gently. She said, **"I am so sorry to call you after I spoke to you so badly, but my daughter needs help and you are the only one who can get her to go get it."** I was speechless!

This woman had called me everything but a **"Human Being"** a few days ago, and had even tried to speak some sort of curse upon me. I told her that I was not going to see her daughter anymore and was about to hang up the phone. But she begged me not to and just wanted me to listen. I did!

She told me that her daughter had been in this ceremony before and it all stemmed from a past drug problem. I said to myself, **"Right."** It was more to this story than she was willing to let me in on. According to her; Tatiana was in grave danger and she needed to check into the hospital to combat this mental issue. She was **"Bipolar"** and had quit taken her medication.

That explained why some months earlier,

Tatiana had told me that she was taken some sort of pills; for what she said was a minor ailment. She said they made her fill worse. She had asked me, **"What would you do?"**

I asked her if she needed it for a life or death situation and she reconfirmed that she was only taken it for a mediocre reason, which was focus! She never said anything about a mental issue. I said, **"If it was me, I would not take it."**

She must have followed my advice. She had stopped taken the prescription and told me she was feeling better. I guess she lied! I felt as if she had just used me for the **"OK."** She desired to fall back into this mind state. I felt guilty and my heart told me to help this girl. It would have been even more of my fault if something else happened to her.

I told her mother I would help. She told me what to do. I just needed to call Tatiana and talk sweet nothings to her!

I would then tell her that I wanted to get married, but only if she agreed to check herself into the hospital. I would meet her there as proof of my sincerity. Her mother said that I was the **"Only Voice"** who could convince her.

I hung up the phone with the island woman and called her daughter. Tatiana answered. *She alternated between anger and kindness, submission and aggression!* I maneuvered through this maze of confusion and convinced her to meet me at a local hospital. She agreed!

The Adventures Of A Drug Addict

Chapter 15
THE HOSPITAL

Tatiana made her appearance at the hospital and called me on the cell phone. She was reluctant to come within its doors; so I would have to persuade. Her mother and aunt had arrived before her and I had met them inside to confirm the details.

All pride and ego was put out of reach. I wanted to at least **"do this"** to help because I had not helped her in too many other ways. I was only her manager!

Her mind was sick and apparently I was wrapped up in her illness as she was mine. I had to see the signs previously, but I chose to ignore her wails of pain. We were living selfishly.

She was already fatally wounded from the life she had come to know and the mother who constantly battered her through control and manipulation! I enabled this break-down of the mind by not being a positive being of **"influential love and compassion."** I gave her the composition needed to enter the world of adult entertainment. We were greatly misguided! I walked to Tatiana's car and got in on the passenger side. She said she was ready to go to the altar, but first we would have to go and rescue her daughter from the clutches of her mother.

I responded by telling her to go inside and sign the proper documents needed to insure that our marriage would take place soon. She said, **"Oh, I get it. We're going to escape and make them think we are dead."** I just agreed with the statement and added to it. She had the look of an excited child. I got out of the car and opened her door.

She jumped out with the energy of an escaped animal. Her arms found themselves tightly gripped around my thin frame. She then proceeded to molest my face with wet violent kisses. It was a struggle to keep her advances in a state of civility but I managed!

We walked inside of the building. We were greeted by two big men who worked there. They were waiting for her in case she became violent.

Upon seeing her mother; she reacted and ran towards her screaming and yelling. The two men immediately intervened on behalf of the island lady. She kept screaming to her mother!

"I'm going to kill you!" The men were about to aggressively restrain her when I stepped in. I told her to remember the plan we had made. She stopped fighting instantly.

A nurse pulled out some paper and she signed it. It gave them permission to help her by any means legally necessary. Before being led to the back by the two large men; she looked at her mother and said, ***"It aint over with bitch!"*** She then blew me a kiss and said, ***"I love you."***

The Adventures Of A Drug Addict

Chapter 16
THE INSANE ASYLUM
&
THE LOUD VOICE

      I made it back to Dallas and started to dismantle my operation of extreme evil! I was ready to put half of it down. The other two girls in my life were still willing to go the extra mile for me! But I had been in and out of the *"self-reflection"* that exists inside of *"contemplation"* for weeks and I was ready to give it up.
      On a Wednesday I received a phone call from Tatiana. It had been almost two weeks since I had promised to marry her. I kept the dialogue short.
      She asked me if I could come and see her on Thursday because it was visiting day. I swiftly agreed and chose to end our exchange of words before she swayed me to change my mind with more chaotic emotions!
      The next day I headed to the address of her new residence; **"The Mental Hospital."** That evening I jumped into my car and went to see Tatiana. I headed to the address in which she had given me. It was not the same hospital as before.
      I walked in not knowing what to expect. I did hope to relieve myself of guilt by hopefully seeing her in a better *"state of mind!"* I got on the elevator and made my ascent to the **"5th Floor!"**
      I stepped off the elevator and walked

passed an armed police. Just a few yards from his vantage point was two huge metal doors. And just beside these two entrapments was a window that secured a nurse who asked, **"May I help you?"** I told her who I came to see and she asked me for my ID.

She told me she would hold it until after my visit. The armed police checked me for weapons and I was cleared to enter. The two doors opened with the identical sound of a jail entry way.

I walked in and was led to a waiting room which would be the place of the allotted meeting. After about five minutes; all of the hostages walked in. It was maybe twenty-five of them in all. Tatiana came to the table where I was posted. She looked very youthful in the eyes, but her skin told a different story. It was as if the last couple of weeks had aged and wore on the biggest organ of the body. She looked like a habitual drug addict.

She sat down and smiled at me. Her head was still tilted like one who can't gather their thoughts. She told me she was ready for our marriage to take place.

I told her to just have patience and stay confined to these walls until I gather all of the resources needed for our big escape. She agreed! I then observed a young Asian lady who had been watching my every word since we had first started talking.

Tatiana's back was facing this lady. Without even turning around; she said with a very angry tone, **"Don't look at her, she is a Satan worshipper!"**

"She put voices in people's head."

The Adventures Of A Drug Addict

She went on to tell me that the last time she was in this place, the same girl was her roommate; just like she is now. She also told me another girl had hung herself in the same room just after talking to this *"so called Satan-worshipper."*

I dismissed this as just talk from one who was mentally ill. Just as she finished saying all of those things; I looked at this lady who had intently focused her eyes on me. Her eyes and my eyes connected in a *"transfer of energy."*

Instantly; all of the people's voices were replaced by the loud and demonic distortion of high pitch screams. I heard the scratching of glass and one overshadowing deep monotone voice of extremely slow speech. I did not understand the words?

However, I did recognize they were not good! After nearly three seconds of *"chaotic sounds of darkness;"* they suddenly stopped. The lady then smiled at me. She turned her head towards her two guests who had been talking to her the whole time as she was scrutinizing me.

I jumped out of my seat and almost fell. Everyone looked at me. Tatiana said, *"I told you don't look at that bitch!"* I thought I was losing my mind!

I told her I had to go and I did not waste any time waiting around for the end of visitation! I told her I would be back next week and kissed her on her forehead. I knew that would be the last time I would see her.

Our short lived partnership was over.

The days of seeing her had come to an end. I left the **"5th floor"** of the hospital where the mental ward was located and descended down the elevator.

I walked out of that building thinking I was committed to seeking change and putting this life of **"pimping, prostitution and drug dealing"** behind me. But the ills of **"Addiction"** and Street life are deep.

I still had not developed the courage to fight my demons and destroy the pains inside of my heart. They were eating away at my thoughts and trying to possess my future. I was now ready to begin my **"Adventures as A Drug Addict!"**

The Adventures Of A Drug Addict

Chapter 17
LOOKING For CHANGE

I had fell into a pit and wanted out! It had been almost a year of living this way and it was **"*Ripping My Soul Apart!*"** I could feel the extreme level of sadness in my heart. I really only desired the family life; the life I had shared with my children for the first three years of their life.

I still felt a great deal of bitterness towards their mother. I had not forgiven her for the way that our family was broken up. This **"*Unwillingness to Forgive*"** produces hate and many other ills!

Every time I received money from one of the girls by way of some cheating husband or boyfriend; I felt empowered! I also had eliminated the emotional factor by having a covenant which allowed any type of intimate male association; as long as it paid!

My lease was about to expire and I had moved in with Maria. I had not heard from Tatiana in over a month and I assumed she was OK. Maria also had become tired from the wear and tear of adult entertainment. I did not encourage her to stay in that arena and she soon retired.

Sarah had moved back to Louisiana. She made the most sales with the marijuana and kept me consistently buying pounds for her to distribute over time. And just as instantly as my income had **"*Skyrocketed;*"** it suddenly **"*Plummeted*"** to the ground! I did not have a source of earnings.

I did not panic nor become depressed. I felt light on my feet. I began to feel as if a great weight had been taken away. I breathed relief.

I felt relieved! I was relieved from not having a relationship with three women of three different types of personality. I felt relieved from not having to spend my time in adult establishments of nudity and perversion just for the sake of the **"dollar"**. I felt relieved because now I could not afford to behave in the way I had come to know.

I started to make jewelry and sell it on the streets since I had become accustomed to **"Hustling for My Wages."** I became somewhat creative in my approach and began locating and buying objects such as sunglasses and fashion jewelry from the foreign owned **"Dollar Stores"** around the metropolis. I would then turn around and sell them for five dollars apiece.

I was lucky to obtain two hundred dollars a week from this endeavor. The revenue was a long way from the nearly seven thousand dollars that was passing through my hands each month on a regular basis. I did not mind. I pushed on! I was feeling free!

The Adventures Of A Drug Addict

Chapter 18
HER NAME WAS ADDICTION

MY new occupation as a *"Street Vendor"* *"Jewelry Maker"* still allowed me to meet new people. I had retired from visiting the adult establishment since I was no longer interested in recruiting girls and identifying myself as a pimp. I also did not have marijuana for sale. I didn't want it anymore or at least that's what I thought!

One night I went out to walk the streets of the artist's district in downtown. It was there I conducted my jewelry business. I brought my friend with me. He was in the same boat and needed money. We walked up and down the street looking for drunken bar patrons to purchase my jewelry.

After about twenty minutes; a girl stopped and became interested in the offer. We told her where we were from and she said one of her best friends was from the same location. She went on to call out the name Lindsey Houston. I said, *"That was my childhood girlfriend."*

She went on to buy one of the objects for sale and I gave her my number to give to the girl that we all knew. Two days went by and Lindsey called. Our conversation was just like the old times.

Lindsey was pretty and always knew it. Her vanity was a level above the average woman but she had some kind ways. We had ended our last relationship; she started to date one of my best friends in high-school. She gave me her address and that night I went to see her. She opened the door and quickly greeted me with a hug.

I was excited to see her. She was still beautiful, but had gotten a lot thinner! Her new look was not hard to get used to.

We sat on her couch and started to talk about what had occurred in our lives since high school. She told me that she had left after graduating and moved to Texas. I asked her what she had been doing all of that time.

She told me that she became a stripper for a few years. After leaving that occupation; she became a **"Hooters Girl."** But now she worked as a make-up artist in the same pretentious location of spending as Maria; the Galleria. I thought to myself, **"This might not be good for me."** I pushed that thought out of my mind.

I then went on to tell her about the life I had just left and wanted to stay away from. Her eyes lit up! I had seen that internal excitement before!

After several hours of talking and smoking; we fell asleep on her bed. I awoke the next morning to the cold treatment of a bowl of cereal because she was an oppressor of the *"culinary arts."* I got back in my car and headed back to Maria's house.

I was seeking the formula for normalcy. I wanted so bad to just fall in love and have a complement in my life who could share in the healing of a troubled heart. Lindsey had the outward appearance of this structure! That next night we made the choice and subsequent failure to move quickly and we were intimate!

I spent most of my time with her over the next seven days. One night she opened up to me about her **"Drug Use!"**

The Adventures Of A Drug Addict

She told me that she enjoys eating *"ecstasy"* pills on the weekend! I smiled because she kept speaking of things I had heard over the last year of my life.

I just wanted to escape my past and I chose to overlook all of those signs! She asked me if I had ever done the drug. I said, *"No."* She assured me that it was safe and it would facilitate so much fun! I started to question her more and every answer came back with answers of sexual fun and partying. I was convinced to try it! I said, *"Damn"* in my mind and that night I made the *"Second Worst Mistake"* of my life! I said, *"YES!"*

Chapter 19
THE NIGHT BEFORE

The law of attraction works in obvious ways! The anxiety and excitement of anticipation was overwhelming. I had always rejected the request of associates to try any narcotic. I did not even like to take over the counter medication. My father; a *"Man of Great Qualities"* had a bout with addiction as a young man and always warned me against any use of drugs.

The life I had come to live caused great *"Self-embarrassment"* and it was obvious to me. I had lowered my ideals and *"Quality of Thought."* I tried to cover the truth of my errors and evil with alcohol.

I reopened the door! And just like a year earlier; I started to meet all of the wrong people! It was time to fall even deeper!

I left Lindsey's house around three in the morning because I had business to handle at 7am; plus my clothes were at Maria's. I stopped along the way to grab a pack of cigarettes. It was there I met a young eighteen year old who was a major supplier of three of the well-loved drugs.

The kid wore *his "Basketball Letterman Jacket."* He told me that he liked my car and said he had just bought one similar. He asked me if I got down. I said, *"Maybe, what you got?"* He told me he had *"cocaine, weed and ecstasy."* He gave me his number and then told me where he stayed!

The Adventures Of A Drug Addict

It was less than three minutes from Lindsey's condo. The next day he supplied me and my new girlfriend with the drug that would take me on a three year journey through the maze that leads to the *"shadowy passageway"* of ***"Drug Addiction!"***

Chapter 20
OUR FIRST DATE

I called the young fellow and went to obtain the promised drug, which would allow me to escape my past. I was anxious! I walked into his *"trap house"* and it was full of customers; some coming and some going. *"Armed Thugs"* with shotguns kept the well-stocked business safe. Their leader supplied me and I left.

I had not eating much that day, so I purchased an order of greasy fish from a fast food eatery around 7pm. Lindsey and I had invited my friend and his girl because they too enjoyed the *"Falsified Bliss"* that the drug offered. I had bought enough for us all. Around nine that night; I embarked on my first date with *"Addiction!"*

We all loaded in the car and headed to a local club to enjoy the mood. We stopped at a 7-11 and bought orange juice because it was the chaser to the *"Pill."* At that store; *I put poison, evil, wasted time and trouble in my mouth and swallowed it.*

We arrived at the club. I walked in and my whole body began to vibrate with the felling of happiness. I felt tingling in and outside of my body.

Lindsey became the most *"Beautiful Person"* to me that night and I just became lost in her eyes. I started to tell her how much I was in love with her. The drug made everything seem better.

The Adventures Of A Drug Addict

This mood of over-romanticism was interrupted by one of the most extreme stomach-churning feelings I have ever had.

I made my way to the restroom located in the back corner of the club. Just as I opened the door; I lost control of my core muscles and started to vomit. I made it to the toilet and set there for five minutes relieving myself of everything that was in my body.

When it was over; I felt energized. Now I had a feeling of power! I had stained my shirt with some of the waste that came out of my mouth, but I did not care. I walked out of that restroom feeling invincible and willing to go wherever!

I went over to Lindsey and kissed her. I told the party what had happened. They assured me it was a normal thing since I had never done drugs. My body tried to reject this **"Deadly poison!"** I made the choice to deny it.

We left the spot around three in the morning and headed back to Lindsey's condo. We stayed up drinking and talking until eight the next morning. The drug did everything she told me it would. The drug made sex seem greater by releasing an **"Overdose of Serotonin"** into the mind! *I fell in love by means of a colored pill which was the size of an aspirin.*

Seven days later; I gathered all of my belongings from Maria's house and moved in with Lindsey. That same weekend we repeated the dance of pill popping, club-hopping, liquor drinking and staying up all night having wild-sex. This is the *"Training of an Addict!"*

Chapter 21
SUPPORTING MY HABIT

I had become *"Addicted!"* I started off just taking half a pill once a week, but now I was doing two twice a week. Lindsey asked me one morning after partying all night if she could help me restart my business of *"drug-dealing and prostitution."* She told me she had experienced doing it all. I inquired further about this matter.

She told me of a wealthy doctor and inventor who was worth millions and had a weakness for her. She wanted to know if I was interested in plotting on him by using her. I listened and from that day forward I viewed her with less respect.

I did not want her to do this because I thought I was in love. I greatly wanted to behold her different than the rest. But she was so willing and I could see it. She began to remind me of all of the others. Our relationship started to decline at that point.

I told her no, but we needed money because our habit required that we spend hundreds of dollars a week. I went back into the business of selling illegal substances to help support our addiction. I bought a pound of weed and started revisiting *"strip clubs"* to push my product.

I ran into a waitress that I knew from months before when I rolled with Chicago. She asked me how I was doing. She sat down and we caught up. She began to tell me about the girls that were working at the club. I asked about their habits and she said I needed to get cocaine if I wanted to prosper.

The Adventures Of A Drug Addict

She told me about her husband and his low prices when it came to the white powder. I told her I had some other ***"Traps to Check!"*** She gave me her number and I told her I would be in contact.

I left and called her a few days later. Her husband sold packages for five hundred and up. I did not have it at the time, so I resulted to robbing someone I had already hurt and help destroy; Tatiana. She still had her wages from her job as a loan officer deposited into one of my bank accounts. I had not touched the account since before her mental break-down.

Her check was loaded twice a month into my bank. I decided to take it. I felt so low just entertaining the idea but I drowned that reality with beer, Crown Royal and the mental notice to quickly put the money back before she knows that it is gone. The next day was the moment of evil.

As a Thief in the night; I went to the ATM machine at midnight and pulled her hard earnings out of my account. It was a little over a thousand dollars. I greedily thought to myself; ***"I have more than enough to get started."*** The next afternoon I added cocaine to my business of drug dealing. I called the lady to arrange a purchase from her other half. I had begun a new chapter in this cycle of being lost!

Chapter 22
POLICE ROBBERY

MY ex-roommate and his fiancé were about to get married and I was one of the groomsmen. I made the five hour drive back home to attend. I brought along an ounce of the high grade green smoke that I sold. It was only for my recreational use for the weekend trip.

His wedding was a blast! He was married in front of his family and his young son. That Sunday I headed back to Dallas.

The drive was smooth for four hours. My car needed gas, so I stopped and filled up. The station had a Popeye's Chicken on the inside and I grabbed a three piece wing order to go!

I only had about forty-five minutes left before I made it back to the city. My cruise was set at sixty-five and I safely piloted my car to the tunes of Marvin Gaye. His hit song; **"What's going on"** was soothing my mind with thoughtful pictures.

I took a bite of the tasty chicken and noticed a **"Yellow Corvette"** had entered my rearview mirror. It was approaching rapidly. I estimated the speed to be around one hundred miles per hour! It passed me like a shooting star.

I shook my head in disbelief because two police cars were parked in the grass dividing the east and west bound lanes of the interstate; one was marked and the other unmarked. The sirens went on and they headed for the speeding bandit.

Both cars instead pulled behind me and signaled me to pull to the side of the road.

The Adventures Of A Drug Addict

Two muscular officers in black bullet-proof vest and gear rushed to my window. One was screaming; **"Let down the damn window."** I did!

With a **"Chicken Wing"** in hand; I asked, **"What's the problem officer."** He said, **"You were speeding."** Those words shocked me! I said, **"Sir, a yellow Corvette just passed you and was going about 100 MPH, but the two of you pulled me over."** He said, **"Shut Up."** He then asked me if I had any drugs in my vehicle. I said no.

He said, **"We are going to search your car because of probable cause."** I said, "What probable cause?" He said **"THIS."** His next action shocked me the least. The officer then threw a single seed onto the floor of my car and opened the door.

The much bigger man yanked me by my arm and pulled me out. A uniformed officer then got out of the marked squad car and directed me to the side of the road. I sat defiant because of what had just happened.

I also had half of the marijuana left over and it was well hidden in the car. The three cops ripped my vehicle apart looking for more than what I had to offer.

They located my **"Registered Gun"** after forty minutes of searching. One of them said, **"We can take you down for this."**

They kept up the hunt and finally found my small stash of pot.

The first officer to introduce himself walked aggressively and angrily towards me. He said, *"Is this all you got boy."* I told him I had just come back from a wedding. He walked away saying, *"This is bullshit."*

The officer with a badge got on his radio and spoke to someone. After about three minutes of uncertainty; a state trooper pulled into the motorcade. He got out of his car and began speaking to the one with the radio. The uniformed officer gave the trooper my information.

The Trooper walked backed to his car! I sat anticipating going to jail! Who would I call to come and get me out? Four minutes of decelerated time passed!

The Trooper reemerged from his vehicle and handed the thief with the radio a paper. The uniformed officer came back to my presence and handed me a ticket. He said, *"Sign it."*

I looked at the ticket and saw that it was for possession of *"Drug Paraphernalia."* It said nothing about the "Concealed Weapon" or the *"Half-ounce of Marijuana."* After only two seconds of examination; I signed the *"contract."*

The "State Trooper" spoke kind words to his friends in crime and left. They laughed together on the side the road. The two muscular guys on *"Steroids"* in bulletproof vests walked passed me to get in their car.

The one who had first spoken to me held up the *"sandwich bag"* filled with *"herb"* and said,

The Adventures Of A Drug Addict

"This is mine boy. Hmm...I'm gonna smoke good tonight." He and his partner repositioned themselves back into their unmarked vehicle with the *"outspoken bully"* at the wheel. He spent their wheels in a hurry to get back unto *"Interstate 20."* The *"soft spoken"* cop with the radio, uniform and badge said, *"This is your luck day, be more careful."* He told me to have a *"nice day"* and he also left the scene.

I was left alone on the side of the road. I sat motionless for the next two minutes; lost in translation! I already knew that cops were just as crooked as the people that they chase; I just had never been exposed to it like this.

They had taken the seats out of my car and had thrown them into the grass. My clothing and boxes of handmade jewelry littered the perimeter surrounding my car. It took me about twenty minutes to repack my things and leave.

I stopped at the store to grab a cold drink because the dry *"Texas Heat"* had de-energized me and I was dehydrated! I opened up the mid-console to get a dollar to pay for what I thought would be a refreshing purchase.

My money was gone! *"The $450 had vanished* into the hands of the police." They had stolen my money! I yelled and screamed every profanity at those crooks. I was so upset! That was all of the money I had. I could not believe it. Another sign of warning had presented itself to me in the form of *"crooked officers."*

Yes, they stole from me and I had stolen from others I dismissed the obvious to continue in my self-created *"Hell!"*

Chapter 23
ME AND MY GIRLFRIEND

The next six months was spent in a cycle of drinking, bars, malnutrition and a very *"expensive drug habit."* Tuesday through Sunday was devoted primarily to the night life. We had our regular spots and that is where we lived.

The distribution operation had failed! I could not keep up with the profits because they all went towards more pill purchases. I eventually gave up.

I started to realize that we were not good for each other. She was an *"Addict"* and now I had become one too. My body would not let me go for long without the High release of *Serotonin*, which only the *"pill of pleasure"* could produce! I stayed on the hunt for a better price and one that would allow me to do more and more of the drug.

Our existence together started to reveal *destruction* within the first month. We both denied truth. We began to argue and she used her words as weapons during times of soberness. *From the outside she was sweet and upbeat; but within closed quarters, she became fury*!

Our life together was defined and enjoyed by the instant-gratification we received from the drug and the war we shared when we were without it.

She had her own trust issues. They stemmed from an absent father and an overbearing mother. She talked about it every time that we flew on *cloud nine*!

Her mother had told her stories about the father she never had a chance to know. She had a picture of him holding her as a baby that she held *"Dear To."* The mom had relayed tells to her daughter about her one-time husband and father to her children.

She told them that he was violent and abusive. Coincidently; Lindsey also relived moments of her childhood. *It starred a controlling, physically and verbally abusive mother.* Lindsey did not go home much to visit her mother. She harbored deep *"Bitterness and resentment"* towards the house where she was kept hostage and the woman who instrumented bondage. *She hated home!*

She visited her mother more during the time we were together than she had in all the years that she had been away. I tried to play relationship doctor, but it was of little avail. I could not convince her of anything. *I had my own issues of pain and mental anguish.* And now I was addicted to a *"$25 Pill"*!

On the third month of my addiction; I looked at her after being up all night *"Rolling"* on our poison and repeating the same dance as we had just two days earlier. I began crying! I wailed to her, *"This shit is going to kill me or send me to jail!*

The Adventures Of A Drug Addict

I got to stop!"
    She paid it no mind. I received a look of disgust and disdain before she marched out of the room. I did not know who to ask for help.

    Our relationship was coming to a showdown that we both wanted. One of us would have to leave or die. That seemed to be our shared view when we weren't under the influence of our ***"Drug of Choice."***

Chapter 24
SUICIDAL RICH MAN

LIndsey had been working as a make-up artist in one of the adult establishments. But secretly; *"She doubled as a Stripper."* She had also started seeing her ex-boyfriend. He too was a low life; *"a cunning lawyer"* with just as much deception in his heart.

I found out about her clandestine job via the revealing phone number. It was littered with glitter and drunkenly written on a card from the adult establishment. This led me to investigate more of this possible deceit because Lindsey had often kept the details of her past secured inside of her mind's closet.

While looking through a box in our apartment; I was confronted with older pictures that showed her nude in sexual fantasies involving multiple men of all races. I understood why she had never had a relationship to last more than a year. *An ex-pimp had fallen in love with an ex-prostitute/stripper who had un-retired!*

I decided to go to the club where she worked to give truth to myself concerning her, me and us. I arrived and decided to wait in my car until more of a crowd had gathered. The married men often start to over-pack the arena filled with nude girls just after getting off of work and just a few hours before their wives expect them home. This is where they could come and express animalism without consequences.

I sat in my car thinking about the more or

The Adventures Of A Drug Addict

less rudimentary words that I would say to her. I was full of resentment and my pride was wounded! It was then that a man parked his new **Black Mercedes** next to me.

The middle aged man sat in the car for about fifteen minutes and then got out and approached my window. I quickly let down the glass to survey his intentions. *He asked me if I could help him get something.* His question took me by surprise because he did not appear to be the type of man who partook in drugs. I got out of the car.

He told me wanted to buy "**100 ecstasy pills.**" The look on his face told me that he was very sad! I needed to know more! I asked him, "**Why?**" The fifty-something year old patron in the high quality suit looked at me and said, "**I have to die today!**"

He then fail to his knees and began to wail sorrows in tear form with no sound; yet yelling violently on the inside! He was grasping my pants leg with one hand and holding his face with the other. **The sight of a man so broken was heartbreaking!**

I knelt down on my feet and consoled the stranger. I put my hands on his shoulders and sincerely begged him to speak to me. He slowly gave in to my request. With help; he was raised up from the hot concrete. His words were intermingled with the **sobs of confusion and hopelessness!** I kept my hand on his shoulder and guided him into openness.

He told me that his latest doctor visit had

revealed a tumor in his brain and that death was promised to him within seven weeks! To make that news seem small; his latest physical to keep the benefits of his multi-million dollar life insurance policy at the large corporation where he worked as an executive was less than four days away.

They would find out about his condition one way or the other by next week. It would be cancelled and **he feared for the welfare of his teen children and a wife whom he loved very dearly.** His only option was an accidental death. *He had devised a plan to overdose on the popular party drug.*

He was a family man to heart and was no patron of this negative establishment of female exploitation. He was trying to take care of his loved ones even in death. I silently prayed for words.

I said, *"Man, there is another way! So you can't give up this quick?"* The non-smoker asked me for a cigarette and I obliged. I asked him if he had received a second opinion from another doctor and he replied, *"No."* His face was blue with despair and his eyes were red with depression. He kept saying, *"Why me?"*

The tears rolled down his face! So much sadness filled the radius between us. He was not ready to die and it was obvious! He just kept sobbing *"Why Me?"*

I began to tell the dying man about my own grandfather who had received similar news

The Adventures Of A Drug Addict

nearly twenty years earlier. He too was given a diagnosis of imminent death. But he did not give up the fight so easy and managed to outlive the doctor's prognosis of a few months by over ten years!

I said, *"He had a family and reason to live and so do you!"* The troubled man began to listen intently as I continued to relay the true story of a southern born gentleman who was also my grandfather. He was a warrior who had done battle with *"death by living!"* His face began to relax and the tears were departed, but his heart was still heavy.

I then opened up to the brother about my own experience and close association to suicide and its ever present effect on my life. I gave a forecast of the future lives of his offspring. I told him that his kids would be left with serious problems if he executes himself.

But, if they are fed truth and allowed to help their father work through this storm as a family; it ultimately would make them stronger and wiser. But the suicide would eventually retard many of their possibilities in life.

Those words entered his heart and took precedence over the fear which wanted *self-inflicted murder.* I asked him what was he going to do and he said, *"I'm not going to die today!"* The man said he was about to go home and tell his family.

He regained his composure and straightened his tie! He thanked me for the words and I told him that I would pray for him and his family. The man tried to extend his thanks to me by giving me the money he wanted to spend on the deadly drugs, but I refused.

I gave the fellow a handshake, pulled him closer and hugged him. I held his hand and softly demanded him to reassure me of his choice to live. He looked me in the eyes and said, **"I'm going to fight this battle!"**

The once shattered man walked to his car with the **"Courage of a Spartan."** His face appeared as a warrior preparing for the battle! His voice wreaked confident hope.

The **"Once Suicidal Man"** of wealth smiled at me and he drove off. He was gone just as quickly as he had arrived. I was encouraged by the event to speak with Lindsey with compassion because we were both in this climate of addiction!

I called her and told her to come outside. She came and I told her that I knew of her dealings with her ex-boyfriend and about her added duty as a dancer. We talked and she said it was only going to be for a short time. I said to her, **"Don't do it anymore"** and she agreed; but I could see the illusiveness in her eyes.

My friend and his girl were going back to our hometown for the weekend. I thought it would be a good idea for us to ride as well. We decided to go in an attempt to put a bandage on the wound of a **"Dead Relationship."**

I was very disappointed at her for regaining her footing in this deviant career path that I had retired from. I wanted out but she kept wanting back in and that is where the **"clash of titans"** takes place!

The Adventures Of A Drug Addict

Chapter 25
DRINKING DRIVING ROLLING

MY friend and his significant other came to pick us up at seven that evening. I loaded our baggage into their car and we began our journey. The expected arrival time would be around one in the morning.

Our first stop was the liquor store. We bought a twelve pack of beer and a fifth of a bottle of hard liquor! My friend had also brought a pound of marijuana to sell upon arriving in our native land.

Our last stop before leaving the city would be to the dealer's house to purchase a party pack of ecstasy pills. We arrived at the location. A young armed thug led us into the drug infested apartment and we bought $150 worth of the narcotics.

It had now been well over three hours and we had not left from under the watchful lights of the city. We made one more stop and rolled up a few *"Cigars"* filled with green bud. Finally we left the town around 10:45 that night.

It had been a long day for everyone in the car. My friend and his woman also had problems of trust and addiction. We now had the solution to our troubles in the form of drugs and alcohol.

We started the party immediately! Everyone dropped the candy like medicine into their mouth and poured spirits into plastic cups! Everything was all right.

The mood was mellow during the ride with small bursts of excitement. The constant fighting and problems of addiction had drained the energy of all passengers!

The Adventures Of A Drug Addict

The girls had succumbed to sleep after only three hours of the five hour road trip.

With their voices out of the picture; I too started to summon the name of *siesta!* My eyes began to lose strength and slowly closed. But I was still conscious of the sounds and environment.

I spoke to my friend, who was also the driver and suggested pulling over. But he confidently responded like only one under the influence can and said, **"I got it!"** I could do no more to fight the weight of my eyelids and at three in the morning I left the helm as his co-pilot! My sight was now obscured by the sleep, but the drugs kept me close to consciousness.

I kept fighting to see the light, but it only appeared in very short segments. It came and went! **The burden of my intoxication was heavy.** Nevertheless, I kept opening my eyes!

The radio was blending into the thoughts of my mind. Then a voice from the song playing screamed **"look"** and I could see again. My friend was sleep with his eyelids lightly sealed!

It took two seconds to realize what I was witnessing. As I was about to tell him to wake up; my vision was directed towards the flashing lights less than fifty yards in front of us. A state trooper stood in the middle of the interstate with his vehicle behind him.

I yelled to my friend, **"Stop!"** He awoke and slammed on the breaks. The car started to slide and it was headed for the officer. He gained control and we watched as it came to a halt less than six feet from seriously injuring or killing the trooper. We were all too over the limit and didn't release any type of emotion.

The pissed man walked to the car with fury In his face. *It was red from fear and anger!* I sat thinking about the pound of grass in the car as well as the left over *"party pills."*

The cop began to beat on the glass and he yelled, *"Let down the fucking window."* My friend slowly let it down and the officer began a six second release of his anger. He said, *"Muthafucker, I ought to beat your ass and then take you to jail and beat your ass some more."*

His eyes said that he wanted revenge! His next words shocked me! He looked at my friend and yelled, *"Get the fuck out of here."* We proceeded to drive past a horrible wreck involving scattered liquor bottles and two totaled cars. The passengers of those two cars did not survive and the wreckage was proof.

I sat thinking and wondering if that should have been us! *How close were we to dying*? My life was out of control in every way and so was theirs! We made it back to our native land and began the cycle of intoxication once again!

I saw another warning go by me! Truth could not penetrate my heart because I was so *"into my addiction and pain."* I had been saved once again by the *"Graceful Hands"* of

The Adventures Of A Drug Addict

"ONE" who had compassion for such a sinful man as me.

Chapter 26
THE FIVE YEAR OLD PROSTITUTE AND SERIAL KILLER

We were staying in a rundown rental property on the east side of town. Our neighbor was an attractive single mother and ***"Bi-sexual Alcoholic"*** who desired the both of us. Her name was Valencia.

Valencia was a woman of promiscuity and daily drunkenness. Her young child acted more like the mother. She would pour her mommy's beer out to protect her mommy from herself.

The five year old daughter spoke to me about what she said was her past life as a prostitute. The time period was the 1860s and she said that she used her career as a sex-worker to murder men. The kid said that she was a ***"Serial Killer!"*** She went on to tell me that she was caught by a mob that tortured and then hanged her in South Carolina.

The little girl would be seen walking and holding the air's hand. *She had long conversations right in front of me with an unseen presence!* She said it was her friend who came to visit her while he was waiting to be born on the Earth!

Her mother said the child began saying those things not long after starting to talk. She said she had taken her to *Psychiatrists and Psychologists who could not offer her any help.* They had put her on drugs that only made her daughter zombie like.

The Adventures Of A Drug Addict

She had taken her young child off of the medication almost a year before.

I began to question the little girl to gain better understanding about this unique personality. She told me that she was sent here to watch over her mother because she was one of her victims during her life as a *serial killer.* She said the only way she could make amends was to unconditionally love and help one of those that she hated and destroyed in the past!

She went on to tell me that she had been born again after her life as a prostitute. The time period was the 1920s. She said that she gave birth to the woman who was now her mother during her late teens. But because of an abusive relationship and heavy *addiction to opium and alcohol*; the child came into the world with serious health issues and died soon after.

The woman speaking through this kid said, **"Losing her was too much for me to bear."** The young girl said that she committed suicide not long after her infant daughter had passed away. She said to me, **"I have to get it right this time because it might be my last chance!"**

She spoke these words to me on several occasions. But because of my own inner conflict and daily battle with addiction; I did not inquire more about this most fascinating character with the memory of one who has lived before. She was on a mission to evolve and to help one whom she had harmed in another time period!

The child was *self-aware of purpose* and obliged to pursue it all the days of her life!

She was a sign and a gift! I wish I had spoken to her more!

Chapter 27
THE RESSURECTION
OF
HATE

I was tired of living in the slums of east Dallas! I began looking for a way out. I had found a better living possibility on the north side of town. I called the middle aged man who was renting the property out.

He answered and I told him of our current living conditions. The man was in a mood of understanding. He began to speak.

He had just gone through a divorce and needed instant money. I worked out a deal with him that would allow us to move in without paying the two months of rent upfront. This opened up the door for Lindsey and I to escape the jungle which was filled with drug addicted street walkers and young thugs aiming to get into trouble!

I had applied for a job and was hired. My first day of work would also be the day that we were scheduled to sign our new lease. We had agreed to meet the owner of the property after I got off of work for the day. The end of my shift came and I anxiously glided my car to what was to be our new home!

I would meet Lindsey and the home owner and we would all certify our intentions with signatures marked on the binding agreement. She was there when I arrived; but the homeowner was absent. I saw keys on the counter and a contract. I asked her, **"Where is the guy?"**

She said that he had to leave in a hurry so she signed the lease without me. I knew that she was lying and I walked out to call the man. He would not answer the phone. She had set me up and I was expecting the worst.

A week went by and we had moved all of our things into our new pad. That Saturday there was a fight. It was during this battle of words that she called the police. *I was not on the lease so I left.*

I came back a few hours later to find all of my belongings outside. I gathered them and headed back east to regroup. I arrived in Louisiana and stayed in my parent's home for seven days trying to develop a plan to get back to the city. I had lost my new job as a result of the break-up.

I felt a strong detestation for Lindsey. I blamed her for me becoming addicted to drugs. And now she had plotted to force me out of the property that I had found for us to get out of the slums of east Dallas. **My fury had resurrected an even greater level of hate for the women in my life; the ones I blamed for my issues.**

I was still years away from recognizing the many faults and character defects that plagued my most inner being. The **"Man in the Mirror"** still had not emerged from his pain!

The Adventures Of A Drug Addict

Chapter 28
THE RISE OF A PIMP

My friend called me that next week to inform me about a girl whom he had met. He told me that she had called him over to the *"Trap House"* where she stayed. He said upon entering; he saw three half naked girls swimming around in cash. I asked for an estimate and he replied; *"about ten thousand dollars."* I said, **WOW; they have to be call-girls.**

He confirmed that all three were prostitutes! I instantly started to plot a way to become part of their reality. **I wanted the money!**

I asked him if there was a male presence in their operation. He told me no. His words were music to my ears. I told him that I would command myself back to Dallas the following day so that I could become a *pimp* again! He laughed and I hung up the phone.

The next day I packed some of my clothes up and headed back to Texas. I made it back into the city with less than one-hundred dollars to my name. I met my friend at the house he shared with his girlfriend and her two young kids.

The three working girls stayed a few buildings away. I told him that we would go and see them later. But first, I had to find a girl to take with me to meet them. I was on the hunt for the pieces needed to rebuild the "machine."

I suggested going out that night and finding someone who would be interested in partying. That individual would be used as a pawn to show off my *"swagger or arrogance"* to the working girls. That type of man was the only one qualified in a **"Whores Mind"** to be her *man, pimp or dictator!*

My friend and I went to one of our favorite bar locations. It was there I met a beautiful young lady who just wanted to hang with me and party. I sat up a date between us for the following day.

That next night we went out to have drinks. I made sure that she had a good time. I paid for the night's expenses. The date left me with only twenty dollars in my pocket!

She did not have a clue that I only wanted to use her to be an ornament or pawn on my side when I went to meet the ladies who had what I really wanted; **A prostitute's money!** My ambition was set! She was ready and willing to be, but I did not want her; **I wanted it!**

I called my friend at midnight and told him that now was the time for my plan to be executed. I told him to meet me outside, so that we could go to the **"trap house"** or the place where **"sex for money"** occurred!

I made it to his apartment! And at one in the morning we headed to the **"Den of Sin"** and **"Currency exchange!"** I was excited and ready. My brain was operating like a stock broker or a corrupt banker.

I told the young lady with me that we were going to meet one of my potential business partners. She was clueless!

The Adventures Of A Drug Addict

We arrived and walked up the stairs. Now was the time that I could see firsthand what my partner had told me about. The possibility of one of those girls **becoming my whore!**

The one that my friend had first met opened the door. Her name was Serene! She was an attractive girl of Puerto Rican descent. She was extremely loud and obnoxious, but very inviting. We walked in.

A very attractive blonde with streaks of pink in her hair stopped us as we were about to have a seat. She looked at me up and down. She said hi to my friend. She then said to the female accompanying us, **"Honey, if you aint come up in here to make some money; you can't sit on that couch!"**

I smiled and I spoke up for the young female character with me who was an unaware part of my design and said, **"We didn't mean any disrespect."** I told the one who had just spoken that we would leave and that I would see her later. I gave her neither rebuttals nor the normal energies that she was accustomed too! I gathered my crew and left!

Part one of my plan had occurred. The girl with me did not understand any of the things that had just transpired. I quickly dropped her off back at her car.

I was creating a drama and I was the director. As we were heading back to my friend's pad; Serene called. She said that she had some green smoke and asked if we wanted to partake. We went back over.

She came outside and got in the backseat of my car. I pulled off and the three of us proceeded to burn the highway while we burnt some grass. I thoroughly inquired about their operation and more specifically about the blonde with the pink streaks.

She told me that her name was Red and that she did not have any pimp in her life. But she said that she needed a man. I asked her about the amount of money that Red made every week and she told me between three and five thousand dollars. Red called her while we were riding and began to ask her about me. We went back to their **"trap house"** and me and my friend was invited back in.

Red met us at the door and this time she had a different approach towards me. She apologized to me for what she called disrespect to one of my girls. I told her that I accepted her apology and that she was right to check my female companion because she was not down.

She smiled at my approval! I stayed at their pad for about an hour. Then suddenly; I looked down at my phone. I told them that I had to go.

Red did not want me to go but I told her that I had business to handle. My friend and I left their domain. I felt that this operation was working smoothly.

The next day Red called my phone. She told me that Serene had given her my cell phone number. We began to talk and I assured her that I was not a **"square."** We talked on the phone for about thirty minutes and I told her that I had to go and handle more business. I did not call back, but waited on her call.

The Adventures Of A Drug Addict

That night around two in the morning; Serene called and said that she and Red would be having a small party. She invited my friend and me to attend. It would only be the four of us!

We went over to their rented suite at one of the higher end hotels. They had alcohol, cocaine, ecstasy pills and marijuana! We began to have a good time. I spoke about many things pertaining to the call girl profession.

After six hours of exhilarating excitement; I said that I had to go. Red stopped me and asked if I would also take her back to their **"trap house."** When we arrived, she asked me to walk her up. I did!

She led me into the kitchen and opened the cabinet. She pulled a well-hidden envelope from between several plates. Her hands opened it and took out green money.

She handed it all to me and said, **"I want you to be my man."** She also said, **"Daddy, that's the money I made last week. But next week will be better. I promise."** I just put the money in my sock without even counting it.

I kissed her on the forehead and said, **"We'll see."** I told her that I had to go and that I would come back later so that we could talk more. I floated out of the door.

I slowly, but aggressively walked to my car. **My ego was boosted** from more negativity. I sat in the seat and began to count the money she had handed me. It was three thousand dollars!

I screamed out loud in my car, with what was then happy joy, but now it's sad regret!

Just a week before my ex-girlfriend had plotted on me and now I was plotting on another. I was back into the game. This time I was more experienced and older. *I had more rage and hate in my heart and I wanted it to manifest into materialism and self-conceit. I was now on the collision course to jail, death or spiritual hell! Only "GOD" could save me from myself!*

The Adventures Of A Drug Addict

Chapter 29
5 STAR DINNING

    The next day was Serene's birthday and her co-workers decided to celebrate. It would be extravagant! Red called me early to inform me that we would all equally chip in to cover the cost of the celebration.
    She had given me three thousand dollars the day before and I also wanted to celebrate my shallow accomplishment of re-entering the arena of ***"Escort Economics."***
    I needed to go shopping! I called my friend to tell him about the execution of the plan and the money I had acquired the day before. Serene had also invited him to be her special guest.
    He could not believe it. He accompanied me on my mini shopping spree because he led me to Red. We walked into the mall and I handed him two hundred dollars to magnify my gratitude for his help! I found what I was looking for in a hurry and so did he. We headed back to his house to freshen up for the night ahead.
    At six that evening; Red called me and said the time was now! My friend and I headed over to their ***trap house.*** We walked up the stairs, knocked on the door and went inside for a seat.
    Red quickly greeted me with a kiss on my cheek and handed me a cigar filled with expensive marijuana. I lit it up and passed it to my friend. He giggled and shook his head with much approval.
    Serene came from the back and said the car was outside. It was time to go. I took another puff of the ***"High Grade."***

We walked out and were met by another blonde and her pimping/drug-dealing man. He introduced himself to me as *Geraldo*. He would become one of my main distributors.

A white Cadillac limo awaited us outside. **In total there were five prostitutes, two pimps and my homeboy.** We climbed into the limo and one of the girls cracked open some Cristal Champagne.

Geraldo pulled out some of the **"High-Grade Marijuana"** he distributed and wrapped some in white rolling paper. He lit it up and we all began getting high. Our next stop was downtown to eat at the five-star restaurant in the sky.

It was the first time I had been **"Balling"** in a limo and the experience made my ego sky-rocket. I was feeling important for all of the wrong reasons! I had gotten ill-gained money from a prostitute and was expecting much more from this weak and emotionally shattered female. My twenty-four year old thinking was severely misguided!

The ride was filled with much inner thought. I had back and forth attitudes about what I was doing. The messages were clouded by pain and resentment!

We made it to the ball in the sky and walked in looking just like the characters that we were. **A pimp looked like a pimp and a prostitute looked like a prostitute!** The upper-class had the look in which you would expect them to have.

The Adventures Of A Drug Addict

They gave us expressions of disgust and we all laughed.

The eight of us were seated and we began to drink! We ordered two bottles of **"Don Perignon"** champagne, priced at nearly $400 apiece. Liquor and beer was also ordered. The dinner quickly turned into a party.

The menu was loaded with unfamiliar entrees that did not sound very appealing. But we ordered food any way. The **"Lobster Tower"** and the **"Wild Boar"** were my choice of eating.

The food arrived and we attempted to eat! Of all the food ordered; only the lobster was ate and shared by all eight members of the party. The other food was not very taste-worthy and was ultimately wasted.

After about an hour; we were all ready to go and start phase two of the party. The waiter brought the ticket to our table. It was given to one of the girls who called out its total to the rest of us. She said, **"$1600!"**

Everyone laughed and agreed that we all had a good time. The price was divided up among the party and we tipped the waiter fifty dollars! Everyone wasted their money living this way.

We all climbed back into the limo and headed back to the north side of town. Everyone was buzzing from the **$800 worth of drinks** in the restaurant. Geraldo had some of the popular party pills that I was addicted to. So, I bought two hundred dollars worth to continue my personal celebration for at least the next four more days.

I had become homeless the week before when I was forced out of the place that I thought would help me start to escape my heavy addiction to drugs and the night life by my ex-girlfriend. I had not spoken to Lindsey since our official break-up. My mind was now focused on my accumulated anger and hate. I was now about to find out why light is void near the ***"Black Hole."***

The Adventures Of A Drug Addict

Chapter 30
JOE THE DIAMOND JEWELER

The next day was Monday and Red had a week long date with her best paying *"Trick!"* We had spent the night before, which was the day of Serene's celebration discussing how she conducted her operation. She began to tell me about the man she called her bread and butter!

His name was *Joe* and he was a *"Diamond Jeweler."* The *Alabamian* had acquired his *"multi-million dollar empire"* through a chain of pawn shops. He loved to spend money on the escorts!

Joe had a passion for diamonds and had spent the last few years trading in the premium jewel! Red had a mini-collection of the choice stone that he had given to her during her trips to see him. She had them wrapped in their proper casings and tucked away!

He was also a compulsive gambler who would fly Red to various *"Horse Tracks"* around the country to perform sexual acts on him and his other rich friends. She received hefty compensation for the moral depredation expressed through male-animalism. She came back from her trips with thousands of dollars and bags full of clothes from high end boutiques.

This time she was flying to Florida. The arrangement in the past had been to pay her at the end of the trip. But I was now involved and I wanted to catch up. *I had to get some of this rich man's money up front!*

I changed his rule. I told her to call him and have him send half via *"Money-gram."*

The ticket price for this visit had been elevated. She called and told him to *"send her two-thousand dollars."* He agreed!

Her flight was scheduled for two that evening; so we headed to DFW airport. But our first stop was by a gas station to pick up the money that Joe had sent to me. She went in and came out!

Two-grand was deposited into my hands! I didn't crack a smile! To her, it appeared to be business as usual! I shook my head with arrogant approval and raised high the volume of the sexist rap music playing in my radio! We kept driving towards the misadventure of **"Pimping, Prostitution and Johns."**

We made it to the airport and Red was semi-safely led aboard the plane! She flew with the wind into more sadness and I drove through the **"fog of darkness"** to find a shady place to stay! I rented a hotel room for the week. I had just orchestrated a master scheme and I had nearly five thousand dollars as proof of this evil.

I began my **"Journey"** deeper into the **"under-world."** I was still a **"Drug Addict!"** But now I had a steady and deep supply of money! I would use this situation to further fuel my anger, aggravate my pain and magnify my sickness. I was adding daily to my own **"Spiritual Impoverishment!"** I was slowly dying!

The Adventures Of A Drug Addict

Chapter 31
THE SECRET SOCIETY: IT'S A SET-UP

    I had spent the next few days locating myself a place to stay. I did not have any credit nor had I worked in almost two years. I had spent the majority of my time being a *"street hustler."* I needed a land-lord who would not do a credit check or seek to verify my employment status.

    I found a town-home in a loud and highly trafficked area on the north side. Coincidently; it was located on a street called **"Mayhem."** The rent was a thousand dollars a month and they needed two months in advanced. I paid the, *"Money talks,"* very little English speaking, Asian woman her money and got the keys to my new place! Everything was moving so fast!

    I had bought five-hundred dollars more of the popular party drug that I was addicted to and decided to go and celebrate that night. I had enough to sell for the night. I was also looking for someone to party with! Red still had not made it back from her business trip, so I did not have to entertain her.

    I took out six hundred dollars from my stash for me to play with. I put a heavy duty rubber band around the cash and slid it into my sock. Next, I loaded some of the party pills inside of the tongue of my shoe. It was now time to journey down town!

    I arrived at my desired location! It was called the ***"Purple Hooker."*** I was dressed in white garments and a hat to match. I was aided in my steps by a cane with a snake for a head. It was not used to soften my steps, but rather my aggression towards the world. The energy surrounding me said, **"Don't Fuck with Me!"**

My alcohol tolerance had been elevated, so I ordered three shots of whiskey and a beer. I had my drink on the outside of the bar. *I was alone with my ego!*

It was overlooking the many club devotees as they came and went in search of one night-stand and greater levels of *"out-control"* and *"drunken behavior."* I was rolling off of the two party pills that I had consumed and also buzzing from the alcohol. It was as if I was waiting for something!

They walked by! Two attractive college girls and their one gay-male friend floated pass me! One of the girls never took her eyes away from mine. Then in a manner of seconds; they had conceded from my line of vision.

Before I could gather my thoughts; the one with the most outer beauty and consumer to the sight of my eyes reappeared! She asked me if I wanted to come with them. I answered yes!

She introduced herself as *Amy*. She said that she was visiting from College Station, Texas where she attended school. I was then assured of a safe and good time; as long as we were together! We walked less than a block to a club called *Space-Lazers*.

We walked in and immediately hit the bar. I ordered a beer for my left-hand and a big filling of long-island ice tea for my right-hand. I was

The Adventures Of A Drug Addict

ready!

She walked in front of me and began shaking her tail feather on my mini-me! I painted pictures with my ego. She was having fun and so was I.

The drugs and the alcohol were energizing me with thoughts of money and schemes to obtain. *I was equipped with my* **Sprint cell-phone** *on one hip and my* **AT&T two-way pager** *on the other.* Both were vibrating with frequent calls from my prostitute who was hundreds of miles away and involved in immoral sexual behavior with old and perverted **Rich White Men!**

My eyes were half-way open while my spiritual receptivity capabilities were completely shut! The loud music and the extra release of Serotonin in my brain from the *third ecstasy pill* I had put in my blood stream filled my empty soul! *Revenge had taken form in the image of a* **pimp** *and* **drug dealer.**

With the windows to my soul securely tucked behind a worthless pair of three hundred dollar shades; I concealed the *ghoul* that lurked on the inside! I was still in the fight, but I was losing. The tidal wave of **"Street-Life"** and **"Drug Addiction"** was not qualified to battle the **"Demons"** of my past! The corruption of my heart was winning the battle to push me closer to self-destruction.

I gazed out into the monstrous audience and saw dances of ancient times. The movements simulated sheep being led to the slaughter! They were the young dead but did not know it!

The sequenced lights offered glimpses into the forces of darkness. *The people were all plotting for the benefit of self-gratification.* So was I!

I wanted those individuals who preyed on others to be my prey. They did not know me or themselves. And I had to eat. Greater levels of evil were out there and they were watching me!

The Adventures Of A Drug Addict

Chapter 32
Mr. MYSTERY
AND
Ms. BABYLON

I held my wooden snake up to the world and began to grove to the beat. My date had stepped to the bar to refill our mixture of *"liquid spirits."* In the distance; I saw a woman point at me and the two walked into my life as visitors from another place!

She introduced herself to me as *"Ideb."* The man said his name was *"Machi."* He began to marvel at my choice of clothing and told me how he loved my style!

I looked at him very disinterestedly because I though he was gay. She immediately spoke up and said, *"He is rich and someone you need to know."* I began to try and focus in on the two strangers!

She told me that he was the owner of one of the most popular male magazines in the United States. She called out the name of her fiancés publication but I had never heard of it. I stood unconvinced!

Amy had reappeared and when she heard the name her eyes lit up! She said to them, *"Are you serious!"* I then began to question the two people before me and who seemed to want something!

The woman named *Ideb* asked to touch my hair and I agreed to her request. Her snow white hands slid between the *"Dread"* that set atop of my head! She smiled in satisfaction!

Her companion began to inform me on their reasoning for being in the city. He confirmed that they were in town to do a photo-shoot for an internationally known musical celebrity. The man named *Machi* was also a photographer for an admired music network.

He then pulled out a technologically advanced camera and showed me pictures of the business he had just conducted. I was amazed to see him, his companion and the famous icon huddled together to form a picture! They were not lying!

After a few minutes of impressing me with material successes; he inquired about the **"*party pill*"** of choice. I told him that I had what he was looking for and would give him one for free if he bought two. He agreed!

He and I walked to the restroom together to affirm the transaction with less watchful eyes on us. Just as we made the deal; a security guard rushed in and began to interrogate us. His bias eyes zoomed in on my ink-filled golden skin and he asked to search me and only me!

He never looked away from my face. All of his attention was on my night-glasses. This bulky man wanted fear from me but I had none to give! I was thinking that I had been set up.

I still had the plastic bag with the remaining ***illegal drugs*** in my hand, so I dropped them to the floor. Just as the man walked closer to begin his mission to find something; *Machi* put his foot over the package containing ***felony charges***. He guided it to a secret location under the litter that decorated the floor!

The Adventures Of A Drug Addict

The guard looked but was unable to locate the *jail time* that came in the form of pills! He apologized for harassing us but said people often deal narcotics in this room! He walked out and so did we. When we got back to the location of the girls; *Machi* surreptitiously handed me the plastic containing the pills that I had dropped to the floor.

The moment told me that it was time to go. It had also stated that I could trust this young rich couple with excess. *Machi* and his companion wanted my phone number and I gave it to them! They had to leave as well. Their flight to another state would be departing in less than two hours.

It was *4am* and time to go! Me and the young beautiful college lady left and went back to my place. We continued the party at my new location on *Mayhem!* I set out and found all that my dark heart was in search of that night.

Chapter 33
Warrants, Jails, Mama & Bail

It had been nearly six weeks since I first met Red and was elevated by her to be her controller and pimp! She had passed nearly ten thousand dollars into my hands. I had spent most of it on my heavy addiction to drugs and alcohol; as well as the places and people such addictions lead a man to!

I had about sixteen hundred to my name and nothing to show for it except my ability to blow money at any given time. My habits were raging out of control and my body lived off of the high negative energy that I fueled it with! I was hooked on so many things!

Red stayed with me at times; but mostly she spent her time at the **"Trap House"** in wait of the next phone call that would reveal the *three hundred dollars an hour* that she charged in exchange for her sexual services! I was living and spending like the cold-hearted pimp I had become. Around seven in the morning; I would get the call to come and pick up the earnings for the night.

I expected anywhere from three hundred to a thousand dollars on any given morning. There were even moments of the occasional jewelry heist that she would pull off and go pawn for its monetary equivalent. It was all handed to me!

One morning I had got a call from Red and she was in the county jail. She told me that they had picked her up on a warrant from two years ago for an accusation of prostitution in another part of the state.

The Adventures Of A Drug Addict

Her *"Get out of Jail Card"* was set at a cash bond of three thousand dollar because she had missed court twice on the same count.

She needed to get out of jail and I only had sixteen hundred dollars left over. I should have had more, but my *expensive drug habit ruled my expenses!* She told me to take three of the loose diamonds that Joe had given her and to pawn them. She had put them in my care after she came back from her last trip with the old perverted Alabamian.

I grabbed the unrestricted stones and headed to the place that had cash for such items. I arrived and was given one thousand dollars for the three precious luxuries! I was now ready to bail Red out of the slammer.

She had four hundred dollars on her when she was arrested! That would be the rest of the bond. I just needed to go to the jail and pick it up. There was only one problem!

I had a warrant for skipping court myself; back when the police had robbed me of my money and marijuana months before. So, she enlisted the help of her mother to collect the remaining funds. I drove and picked up the woman who could do nothing to protect her little girl from the ravages of prostitution!

I arrived at her mother's house and had a chance to meet a woman who had gone through change, but could not extend the same levels of healing to her child. She told me that she was happy that I was her daughter's new *"man"* because the last pimp in her life had beaten her into the hospital several times! He had also kept Red away on road trips for months at a time and did not allow her to contact her family!

Her gratitude came as a surprise to me. I didn't expect to hear her mom praise me for being her pimp; but I understood her logic. Many of the men that I had met through my intimate association with this illicit activity were violent towards the women involved!

She began to tell me where Red's life had gone wrong. Her alcoholism and drug addiction had affected her daughter horribly and so did the man whom she once loved! He had repeatedly sexually molested Red as a little girl and she never healed. Mom felt regret! The sadness in her eyes told the story of a parent hurting deeply for the child that she helped ruin!

We made it to the **"Bail Bondsman"** and her mom signed the paperwork to get her daughter out of jail for prostitution yet again! I felt disappointed in myself but did not let the thought direct my mind towards reflection. The sooner Red was out; the sooner she could hit those streets and gather us more money! That was who I had evolved into!

The Adventures Of A Drug Addict

Chapter 34
THE
FAMOUS CLIENTELE

Red made her way out from between the security of metal bars! Without further ado she began working to gather the money we had lost in paying her bail. She was also in need of a lawyer to represent her on the charges of prostitution. The next two weeks were spent doing just that.

One morning Red had called me to pick her up from a neighboring community of prestige! I had taken my friend along with me because Serene was with Red on the date. He and Serene had become party partners, but not more.

We made it to a gated community with an armed security guard protecting the only entrance into a neighborhood landscaped with multi-million dollar homes. I gave him the name of the house where the girls were at and he called. This particular client of Red's became well known for being the free loading house guest of a very infamous acquitted murderer!

He gave permission and we entered his bubbled world. We drove through a maze before coming to the house that he occupied. It was a huge three story mansion overlooking a lake. An outside party balcony surrounded each floor. All three levels had evidence of a wild party the night before!

I called Red and they came out. After getting in; we descended from the heights of luxury back to the **"Trap House."** She was tired but ready for more!

Red pulled a thousand dollars from between her breasts and put it in my hand! She and Serene had split the total, which was *two thousand*. I counted it and gave her back fifty to get her nails done. She kissed me on my cheek and went inside to rest.

It was 9am on my clock and I wanted to start medicating myself early. I spent the next ten hours of my day getting intoxicated and dealing drugs in the strip-club. Red was filling sick. So I told her to take the day off and recover.

I went and got her from the *"Headquarters of Their Sin"* and brought her back to my place. She slept on the air-mattress inside of my unfurnished *"House of Drug Addiction."* I gave her cold medicine so that she could hurry and get back on the job. The next day she was healed from her sickness and gave herself the OK to go back to work!

The Adventures Of A Drug Addict

Chapter 35
THE GLOOM OF ADDICTION

I was out of control! As a wave of the sea; my physical body was being tossed to and fro, backwards and forwards. And just like the water in the ocean; I could not escape from that which I had created and was contained in! Red had given me the resources that I needed to blaze myself a path to ***inner hell!*** I spent all day and night on the verge of total collapse!

The drugs and alcohol had taken me over! I did not know who I was! But I did realize that I was an addict who was addicted to the dramas that my addictions imparted!

I spent my afternoons conversing with girls working at the strip-club. I had recently met a dancer named ***Candy*** at one of the nude enterprises and who happened to stay right down the street from me. She was now helping me push some marijuana and ecstasy pills to her fellow workers, and the men who came to watch them perform.

She had a ***crystal-meth habit*** and used the money that she made to do just that. I had elevated my commitment to drug addiction by allowing more and more drug addicted people into my life.

I hardly ate! The constant grinding of my teeth had started to corrupt my smile. I needed the comfort of the pill to allow me to love for a moment, and the encouragement of the alcohol to let me be this person who I was not! It gave me release from the pain that I had let defeat me! *I was screaming loud to no one for help and it was no one to help!*

My nights were spent in the company of lost girls who sold themselves for the comfort of their addiction! It was done to escape their past of *sexual demoralization and abuse!* We were all in the same boat; *the pimp and his prostitute were the same!* Both had fallen victim to previous experiences from lifetimes before. And just as you; they were both people once upon a time!

I was taken more and more chances everyday by building up my resistance to the life! There was a very thin veil between me and death! Overdosing was something I thought of constantly and rest had become a distant past!

I only slept when my drug filled vehicle or body shut down because of a near absolute exhaustion of energy! Arrest was something I had come to expect one day. I just wanted to get as much money as I could before that day. But I could not save a dime because of the evil attached to the currency at hand. *And the truth is that addiction demanded my all!* I was not safe being me!

Chapter 36
THE FALL OF AN ADDICT

It had been three months since I had met Red and she had given me thousands of dollars from her career as a *"call-girl."* Our meeting had sky-rocketed my **"Drug Addiction"** to that of a potential fiend if I ran out of money. I was spending a grand or more every week on the details of my habit!

Machi and his fiancé had wanted to take me under their wings for one reason or another. I had not seen them since our initial and only meeting; but they frequently called me from foreign places around the globe and let me speak to some of their famous friends. It was as if we were all best buddies from years ago.

They invited me to travel with them but I was still hesitant about the rich couple of amazing excess! They had informed me that they would come and celebrate with me on my birthday, which was about six weeks away. I looked forward to dangling with the mysterious pair!

I had more grave concerns to attend to; such as my business of drugs, prostitution and addiction! I had no time to dwell on possibilities outside of the bubble that I had put myself in. Something was about to happen!

Red had recently told me about a friend of hers who was also a prostitute. She was about to get out of jail. She also stated that this girl was a money-maker. She would go and pick her up and bring her to me as a present upon her release in two days! I was about to inherit another girl who could also bring in six to ten thousand every month. The thought of more cash excited me!

The next morning; one of her other fellow call-girls came to pick her up to make the trip to Houston. I gave her a few hundred dollars and she was gone! Greed energized me over the prospect of more!

The day went by and I did not hear from Red. I called her phone but there was no answer. The girl who ran the **"Trap-House"** had not heard from her either. One day turned into two days and three into four. Eventually a week passed by and it was as if she had just disappeared.

When I called; her cell-phone always went to voice-mail! I went by her mother's house but she had not heard from her either. I was worried! Was she dead or was she in jail? I did not know! I called the various lock-ups from Dallas to Houston trying to **locate my missing prostitute.**

That did not stop me from going out every day and spending lots of money on the club, alcohol and my various drugs of choice. A month went by and I had exhausted my funds on everything and everyone! I only had six hundred dollars to my name and I was spending several hundred every day. **I began to panic!**

I took the diamonds that Red had left at my place and sold them. I only got four hundred for the two imperfect stones that I had. My drug distribution operation had soured because it was only used to minimize the cost of my habit!

It was time to pay rent and so I did. **My cash was gone and I was turned into a fiend!** I could not believe it!

The Adventures Of A Drug Addict

My birthday was coming up and *Machi* and *Ideb* had promised to visit and help me celebrate my coming into the world. I needed a pick me up and an opportunity to binge. They told me that it would be an unforgettable experience!

Chapter 37
IN HEAVEN DANCING WITH DARKNESS

I had witnessed a total collapse! Red had vanished into thin air and taken with her the money used to supply my addiction! I had lost my business again. My friend and his new stripper girlfriend were staying with me but I felt alone!

However; it was my birthday and I had come across a few hundred dollars as a gift. I quickly went and bought a pack of ten ecstasy pills for the night. *Machi* and his complement were coming to see me and I expected to have a great time.

He had called me two days before and informed me that his fiancé had a mild stroke! He acted as if that event was insignificant. *Ideb* took the phone from *Machi* and began to insure me that she was alright. She also said that she was ready to have a good time on the drugs that I had bought!

I didn't understand the significance of their comments at the time; but I did perceive it to be strange that a twenty-six year old female could have a stroke and go to party two days later!

The night came and it was time! My phone began to vibrate with a call from the duo! I answered and they met me. I got in the car with them and began my journey into an unforgettable night!

I gave them each two party pills and we rolled! Our first stop was to a club on lower Greenville; where many such places were bunched together. We walked to the door and *Machi* told the doorman who he was.

The Adventures Of A Drug Addict

The owner came to meet us about three minutes later and we were led upstairs to a private area. He gave us a bottle of expensive Champagne and said that the drinks were on the house. I began my descent! I landed on the dance floor.

We all began to move to the music. *Machi* and *Ideb* were into the drums and I saw them bend their backs in ways that did not appear possible for humans! It looked as if the many colors of light vibrations grouped around them!

The effects of the alcohol and the pills that the young people call *"skittles"* had taken over my body! No traces of insecurity existed! I was rolling at *"mach-speeds."* My eyes were securely tucked behind my night-shades to cover the evidence of the effects of the potent drugs on a *"man."*

It was near closing time, so we decided to go. We needed to meet my supplier and pimp friend Geraldo to get more pills! I set up the meeting!

His mobile distribution business was at a popular hotel known for prostitution and drugs. We met him at the store beside of the location and got gas and waited for his arrival. His Lexus pulled beside us and I got out.

I paid three hundred dollars for another pack of ten pills as well as a little marijuana. He said he had something to tell me and began to speak. According to his prostitute and worker; *Red had been taken by her former pimp and forced to work for him!* He told me that the girls were working on a plan to get her back, but first she had to be found!

I thought to myself, ***"This is too much!"*** His words had put me in a state of shock and relief for a moment! I changed the subject to a lighter note.

I began to question him about a place that my friends and I could go to and keep our party going. He excitedly told me about a setting that stayed opened until noon the next day! He said the crowd was one of all types of people and that everyone would be feeling like us! I asked him the name of the place and he said,

"Heaven!"

The Adventures Of A Drug Addict

CLUB HEAVEN

We arrived at *"Heaven!"* It was situated on a dead end street in a warehouse district. It whereabouts was unknown to the general population. From the outside it appeared to be just another place of business. But then I walked in!

Just as the three of us entered; I observed a young man whose eyes were in the back of his head as he lay on a couch by the entrance. *Machi* told the guy at the door who he was and we were exonerated from a fee. We then entered another world.

It was unlike any bar or club I had ever seen. There was not just one space but many dark rooms with couches and reclining chairs to aid the various drug abusers. There were characters. Many people were just lounging and having intimate conversations. There were white and black, straight and gay people. The crown was very liberal. We walked around to absorb the environment.

From room to room the energy was surreal! We all sat down and began to just intake the feel of our reality. The couch that we sat on was surrounded by other similar sitting comforts.

Just as we sat; a guy dressed in the Halloween costume of a *"bumble-bee"* came and asked if we wanted to see the greatest light show on the planet. His garments screamed; I am extra-ordinary. *I told the creature yes!*

He began to make his hands move and the

lights started to dance around him. After about five minutes his show was over and he moved around. It was entertaining to see a chubby gay-black-guy dressed as a bee doing a light-show!

We set for a while longer and began to move around. Machi had started to complain about the light coming from a lamp that was close to us. He kept saying he did not want anyone to see him in the light.

We came to another room and had a sit-down. *I observed young college students selling cocaine, meth, special-k, pills, weed, mushrooms and acid in plain view and for all to see.* They were pocketing hundreds of dollars every few minutes!

I instantly knew that I could come back here when I had something to distribute and get back to making the money needed to supply my lifestyle of *addiction to drugs, women and clubs!* I did not know how I had never heard about this place. But I did know I was happy to know where *"Heaven"* was!

Machi got up and began to walk around. He did not reappear for almost two hours. I and Ideb walked into another room with fewer people and less action. The inhabitants of this space were all love bugs caught in the expressions that serotonin and sexual energy encourage. We sat on the floor in the mist of about thirty chilled out and less excited couples.

I asked her about Machi. She said, *"Don't worry about him."* She then began to stroke my ego with words about my physical beauty and apparent mysticism!

I didn't know how to take this information from

The Adventures Of A Drug Addict

the fiancé of the man who was not around.

Ideb then said to me, **"I can show you things inside of your being that you do not know exist."** I asked her what she was talking about. She told me that I was special and that they have been watching me! I looked at her with perplexed eyes and said, **"Who has been watching me?"**

She said, **"I will show you where they are from!"** The first instruction was to trust her and to trust myself. I just went with it!

She asked to see my right hand and then placed her left hand on top of it. She then told me to hold my left hand close to the ground on which we were sitting atop and concentrate. I did as she told me for maybe two or three minutes.

I began to see visions of outer-space inside of my closed eyes. My stomach started to send signals to my brain that it was nauseating and all strength left me. I felt like I was dying and was close to losing consciousness!

It was during this moment I heard a male voice say, **"What the fuck is that on the ceiling?"** I opened my eyes and looked! The sky above our heads had turned into the spectacle of universe phenomena!

Everyone in the room **saw comets** shooting across the space in the room, diminutive **blazing stars** and other space bodies. It was as if we were **flying in outer-space.** The very colorful and highly beautiful images had also taken over the very walls that surrounded us!

The same guy who had first noticed the manifestation of the unknown looked towards us and said, *"It's coming from her!"*

I looked and *Ideb's* right hand was raised to the sky *like a wizard!* Energy was flowing through me and out of my right hand and into her body. It was then passing out of hers. It was exiting her right hand, through her fingertips and then forming a tornado like cloud as it overtook the ceiling!

I jerked my hand from the woman when she looked at me and smiled. I gazed at her in disbelief and great uncertainty! The event had me coughing for lack of something and feeling a great weakness in my mind!

The people in the room began to talk and all questioned what they were seeing. One girl came up to *Ideb* and asked her how did she do that? She told the girl that if she hanged with us; she would show her more.

She told me that it was time to go and helped my life-less body unto its feet. As we walked out of the room; *Ideb* put her palm about a foot from the wall and held it there. I witnessed *electricity shooting from her* hand like a sci-fi movie!

Ideb said, *"The darkness is filled with mystery."* We left the scene of the incident being harassed with questions of how! The party goers thought it was part of some show or maybe they didn't; but I knew something real and unexplained had just happened.

Machi, who had been missing for hours, was found moments after. We all journeyed back

The Adventures Of A Drug Addict

to my place to keep on hanging out. The girl who *Ideb* had promised to show other seeming miracles too came with us, along with her boyfriend.

The feelings from the drugs were gone. I was left with my thoughts. During the twenty minute drive back to my place; I reflected on the events I had just witnessed and been part of.

We made it back to my place. My friend and his stripper-girlfriend were there. I told him that I needed to talk to him upstairs.

He and I walked to my bedroom and I began to tell him about the things I had witnessed. He couldn't quite understand but he did see the look in my eyes. He trusted that something powerful had occurred.

We walked back down and *Machi* began to tell us stories of how he had come into riches. *Ideb* set beside me and leaned her head on my shoulder. He then went and got a box from his truck and pulled out a necklace.

As he pulled the jewelry from its protection; our eyes fell into a **hypnotic trance** and we viewed the most elaborate display of stones. The size of it was big and the weight was heavy to accommodate the many rocks that it housed! ***It was made out of gold and decorated with diamonds, emeralds and other precious gems of every kind.***

Everyone said *WOW!* He said it was very old and to me it looked like something not from this planet! He then put the special object back into the case and the trance was over.

My friend and I looked at each other in

amazement. **Who were these people?** *Ideb* whispered to me and asked if I would escort her outside and I did. The temperature was in the mid-thirty's and **she was barefooted, sleeveless and wearing shorts.** I stood with her while I smoked a cigarette. I became cold and went inside.

I went to use the restroom and when I came back I saw her perform the impossible again. She was still outside and the girl who had come with us was looking out of the window at *Ideb*. I went and looked out of the other window. I saw her spinning around in a circle and the leaves were doing the same thing around her radius; like a tornado. **She then suddenly stopped and the suspended leaves fell to the ground.**

Ideb looked at the windows where our eyes had been observing her and she smiled at me again. I closed the curtain like one may see a character do on a movie, and so did the girl. We looked at each other and our mouths dropped in an attempt to primitively communicate a feeling to one another.

Ideb came back in and said she wanted to go lay down. *Machi* said that it would be fun to take a nap with her! The comment was very unusual!

She wanted me to show her the way. When we got to my bedroom; **she asked if I would stay for a while and I did.** She then asked me to lie down beside her on the bed and I did.

The Adventures Of A Drug Addict

It was like I had falling under her control and I knew it. I found her hand on my thigh and she began to massage it softly. She then started to ask me questions about me coming with them when they left.

I told her that I could not come with them because of my finances. **She said that they were rich and would take care of me in all ways.** Her next questions took me by surprise when she asked to kiss me. *Machi* was down stairs and that was something I did not do.

I said no! But she tried for the next few minutes to seduce me. I eventually got up and walked back down stairs. It was something very strange about the way this lady kept trying!

It was about six in the evening and *Machi* said they were about to go to the store. Him, *Ideb* and the girl who came with us from **"Heaven"** left for what should have been a ten minute expedition. But they never came back. We waited and waited.

I called *Machi's* cell phone, but I got no answer. The boyfriend called his girlfriend, but he did not get an answer from her. Two hours had passed by and I told him that he had to leave.

Everyone was gone and I went back upstairs to lie down on my bed. I turned off the lights in my room and realized that the empty space was illuminated with a red glow. I went to turn back on the lights but all three had blown out at the same time; as if to say, **"You will see this."**

Just as I looked outside, I saw that the moon was full; a concentrated **red glowing light** in the sky shot between my vision and the moon. It vanished quickly. I went back to the bed and put my confused body back on it.

I laid there and just set in thought about the past twenty-four hours and its significance to my life. **What had I just witnessed?** Who were they? Why had they disappeared and wasn't answering their phone? What happened to that boy's girlfriend? **How did Ideb do that to me in "Heaven?"** Was it real? If it wasn't; how did the other people see the same things that I saw and my body had felt? **Am I losing my mind?**

Why is the room where she came to lay glowing with a red tint? What was the red glowing object that I just saw in the sky? It was too many questions that I could not answer, but I knew who could and they were gone!

I never heard from these two entities again. I called and never received an answer. The phone number was disconnected a week later and all traces of those two people vanished that cold day in December!

As they were walking out of the door to go to the store; *Machi* told me to search google for **"Machiavelli the drug-dealer."** He said it was important information there for me. I found that, but not them!

The Adventures Of A Drug Addict

Chapter 38
LIVING AS A FIEND

I spent the next month in a constant performance of get and try to get! I needed money to live like the addict that I had become. I would pick up a half-pound of weed and sell it just to support my extreme dependence to the ***"pill!"***

The amount of money that I was spending had caught up with me! My most trusted supplier used to consign to me. However, I owed him cash and did not have it to give. My Consignment days were over.

The weeks started to move at a slow pace. My thoughts became preoccupied with the past. Financially; I wasn't keeping up with my addiction!

Within a few months I had lost my place; the $1000 a month rent was too much for a ***"Drug Addict"*** like me to afford! I dwelled like a transient. My flesh stayed in between friends and hotels.

I still had connections with a few girls that I knew; they would semi-help me get off of my various illicit products. They liked me and were willing to do a lot of things. **We were mentally sick and spiritually lost;** we only used each other for what we could get from one another.

Nothing was more important to me than my need for the ***"pill!"*** My life force had become entangled with the dramas attached to it! I was sinking faster than ever.

I finally had some luck and came across two grand. I used the money to buy a few hundred of the party pills and some grass in hopes of bringing my lifestyle back to what I had come to know; even if for only a short period in time! It was time for me to go and set up my store in **"*Heaven.*"**

I arrived into the underworld of addiction and descended into **"*Hell*"** with two hundred pills to move. It was my first time back to this place since the unworldly experience with *Machi* and *Ideb*. I did not know what to expect, but I did expect to re-gather the money I had spent on the pills and even more!

I brought two of my associates to help me distribute the drugs! We stepped into the den of **"*inner demons*" and "*unresolved emotional issues!*"** Within a few hours; all of my pills were gone except about ten. The rest were reserved for my personal use.

My associate came up to me when it was time to go and told me that a girl wanted to buy the rest of my product. I told him no, but he insisted that she was willing to pay me double for what I had. She then walked up and introduced herself to me.

Her name was **Stacy.** She was a **twenty-two year old multi-millionaire and computer-genius.** She had gotten rich by selling a tracking device that she invented. It is used in cars around the world.

She also had the most extreme addiction to drugs that I have ever seen. She begged me to sell her my remaining supply; but I refused!

The Adventures Of A Drug Addict

When that did not work she invited me to come and be her guest at her house. I accepted.

I wanted to stay just a little while longer and take in the energy of *"Heaven."* I sat down on one of the couches in the dark room. A man with a French accent asked me for a cigarette. I gave it to him and he introduced himself to me. ***His name was Harry and he was lawyer.***

He and I conversed about many things during this twenty-five minute hiatus on the couch. He asked me about some marijuana and I told him that I had what he was looking for. I gave him a sample.

He wanted my number and I also granted him that. He said that he did not have many friends and wanted to get to know me. I told him to call and our conversation ended.

It was time for me to go. I walked back over to the one called *Stacy* and told her that I was ready. It was then that I saw *Geraldo.* He stopped me and pulled me to the side. He told me to watch *Stacy*. He had heard that a guy whom she knows had been sent to jail for a long time for drug distribution; and she may have had something to do with it.

I assured this colleague that I had it under-control and not to worry. And without further ado; I ascended out of *"Heaven"* with *Stacy*!

Chapter 39
DYING YOUNG

I followed *Stacy* to her house in a far north community outside of the city. It was eleven in the morning; and the **"Vamps"** had been up all night and was looking for more! She lived among other well to do people; maybe not as young, but still well to do.

I parked my car behind her house. It was a two-story house worth hundreds of thousands. I walked in as the only man of color in the house of about eleven.

She invited me into her room. ***It was filled with hanging sex objects that said bondage!*** There was psychedelic paint that filled the wall with unconscious thoughts of drug use!

We sat on the bed and I did not know what to expect. I gave her two of the pills and she quickly **"crushed them."** She followed that by **"snorting them"** up one of her nostrils." She said that it goes into the bloodstream faster.

She poured herself a drink and began to try to sexually molest me. Her attempts were thrown off course by a knock at her door. It was one of her roommates who only used her for the obvious.

He wanted the keys to her SUV and some money. She gave it to him and he left. But in the process; he presented her mind with the realization of a cycle that has been part of her life for many years; even before her recent

The Adventures Of A Drug Addict

accomplishment of becoming rich.
    The drugs began to kick in and she began to put out her feelings. Her words echoed the pain of **dying young and not being loved!** I listened as raindrops poured forth from her sad eyes!
    She said that she couldn't own a computer because **she had hacked into one of the government's agency** a few years back. She and some friends only did it for fun. However, it eventually caught up with her when the **FEDS came to her door and she was arrested.** She said they gave her a choice of either working for them or going to jail for twenty-five years. She said that there was no other option!
    They moved her to a community in the mid-west where others who had been similarly **tracked and caught** also lived and worked for the government. She had three years of what she called forced labor. Upon release; she was forbidden from ever owning a computer again.
    When I had first entered her house; I observed several computers that appeared to not work. I asked her about what I had seen and she gave me an answer. She said that she bought a couple of computers every month. When she had gotten maximum use out of it; she submerged it into water. That was the way to destroy the hard-drive and ensure that she was not linked to its use.
    I listened in amazement as she told me about her "**gift!**" She said that she sees language when the computer is turned on. According to her; she knows how to talk to it and

make it do anything that she wants it to.

She then told me that **she had lupus!** It was **killing her slowly** and causing her much **physical pain** in the process. The tears started to rain again from her face!

"The drugs help lessen my pain!" She miserably said; *"But only if they are done in high doses!"* The average was **70 ecstasy pills a week** she said. At times the drugs were *injected into her rectum* and other times into her feet and eyeballs.

She said that allowed the drugs to give her even greater relief from the physical and inner agony. I felt sad for this woman. I dried her eyes with my shirt and was overwhelmed with compassion for this troubled girl. *We both cried*.

Her cheerless words did not stop there! She said that her father also had taken advantage of her. He had tricked her into buying a used car dealership without giving her any ownership. They had an estranged relationship that she obsessed over because he was her only family.

I stayed at her house for about three days. They did massive amounts of drugs! No substance was off limit. Crack, heroin, pain-pills, sleeping-pills, uppers and downers; they did them all!

Stacy paid for everything; thousands spent on drugs and thousands spent on alcohol. We drove to the music store on one occasion and she bought equipment for whoever was with her that day! **She was a sucker** to her people and

The Adventures Of A Drug Addict

they took her for as much as they could get. T
    She also sponsored the drug business of one of the guys who stayed with her. He had run out of his supply of drugs the morning that I met her. That was the reason she was trying to buy from me. With everything that I had learned about Stacy; I decided to keep in touch. We met in **"*Heaven*"** but we were headed to the **"After-Life."**

Chapter 40
HARRY: HEIR TO THE THRONE

I left Stacy's house and went to rent me a hotel for the next two weeks. It had been four days since my last trip into **"Heaven."** I got a call that Thursday morning from the lawyer I had met there.

In a heavy French accented voice; he said, **"This is Harry."** He went on to tell me that he would like to meet somewhere for coffee and to buy some weed. I agreed. The designated location was Seattle's famous coffee house at six that evening.

I arrived and found Harry sitting out front. I went and shook his hand. We then walked in together and ordered a jolt of caffeine. We made our way back outside and had a seat.

He spoke with his **Ray Ban sunglasses** hiding his eyes. Harry said that he could not trust people because of his family's background. He went on to tell me that I was the first man of color that he had ever befriended.

I assured Harry that I did not care about his family or his profession. He then asked me if I wanted to go back to his house and smoke some of the green herb that he was buying from me. I agreed.

I walked to my car and he to his. I observed that he was driving a new **$130,000 Porsche.** I just attributed it to his career as a lawyer. We drove down the street into mid-town and pulled up to a high-rise. Harry gave the **valet his keys** and got in with me. He directed me to pull into the parking garage.

The Adventures Of A Drug Addict

I pulled my ten year old car into a garage full of names like **Mercedes, Porsche, Aston Martin** and other very expensive foreign vehicles. The car was soon parked and we headed to the elevator to make an ascent to his **16th floor home.** With my tattoos exposed and my eyes speaking truth; *everyone noticed me as I floated through Luxury.*

He invited me in and we walked into his eight-hundred square foot pad. It was clean and neat with **Modern European Furniture**. The carpet said that not many people walked on it.

We sat down and Harry began to talk. He told me that he was working for one of the biggest and best known law firms in Dallas. He had a salary of about two-hundred thousand a year; which was good for a thirty-one year old sophomore in law. *He was also a pilot with a plane and a classically trained musician!*

I began to wonder how someone just out of law school could be so much. Harry pulled a small mirror from under his couch. It had thin lines of cocaine in rows and a twenty dollar bill rolled tightly atop it!

He asked me if it was alright with him **"Playing with His Nose"** and I told him, "Cool"! The paper currency was turned into drug paraphernalia when he put it inside of his nostril. He put it to the glass and sucked a line of the dirty white powder.

That one was followed by two more and he was talkative!

Harry asked me if he could open up to me and I told him, *"Yes."* He said that he had a secret and wanted to share it with me. I lit the joint that I had brought with me and told him to talk.

He said that he was very rich.

That did not surprise me because of his love affair with planes. It did surprise me when he told me that he was one of the heirs to an old ***"European Wine Dynasty"*** that included an ***expensive gold champagne bottle!***

Harry pulled out pictures and began to show me evidence. His dad was once a Diplomat in the United States from France. He was worth millions just by blood and had access to hundreds of thousands.

He said that he had never met anyone like me and just wanted to get to know me. I told him a little about me and he was ok with it. He took another hit of the snow and got up to get us a beer.

I asked to go to the restroom and he pointed the way. My hands opened the door and I saw **Rolex** and other expensive watches on his marble counter top. He had over **$50,000 worth of watches displayed in elegant form.** He really was rich.

He and I left his place after about three hours of getting to know each other and took a ride in his expensive vehicle. We headed to the nude-establishment where his girlfriend worked. I got to see another side of his character.

The Adventures Of A Drug Addict

Harry had been very sheltered and over-protected. His social skills suffered because of his childhood isolation. He was searching for an edge and he had found the embodiment of it in a *stripper named Geneva!* She was more of an addict than him and he loved her. She did not reciprocate the feelings and I observed his ignorance on this matter.

He became one of my friends after this first meeting. He taught me about pretentious society and I relayed common-sense to him. We were both playing the insane word *"Sport of Addiction."*

Chapter 41
THE AFTER-LIFE

No amount of money was enough to sustain my craving. I sold drugs simply to do greater amounts of the vices in which I was addicted to; *alcohol, ecstasy pills and clubs.* My life was an embarrassment to myself and I was a shame of who I had become.

I spent the next two months on the biggest binge I had ever been on. I wanted to stop everything, but I had made something bigger and stronger than me. Who was I?

My father asked me to come home for a while. He suspected that it was much that I was hiding and going through. I left the city life behind and ventured back to the country. There was only one problem; *I brought along one hundred and fifty of the party pills.*

I popped them all and when I ran out I began to fiend for the remedy. The money was gone that I needed for my drug lifestyle. *The mind starts to react and the body begins to ache!* It was calling!

Harry had become one of my hang-out buddies. He called me two days after I ran out of my drugs. He wanted me to meet one of his famous friends. He also liked to make the *"Girls go Wild."* The two of them would be flying back to Dallas the next day, which was a Saturday. We would all party and have a good time.

It was perfect timing because my body was getting sick from a lack of the *"sustenance"* that it lived on.

The Adventures Of A Drug Addict

I called *Stacy* and told her that I would be coming back into town. She kept the drug that we both were heavily addicted to and I told her to have me about ten of them; because I was not well.

My corpse had been absent from its energy source and I couldn't take it any longer. ***I needed it.*** Three days was the longest I could be without the love of the pill!

I awoke that morning and packed my belongings into my car. I did not tell my family that I was leaving because they would have tried to stop me. Instead; I wrote them a letter and illustrated how much I thanked **"GOD"** for having them in my life and how much I loved them! There were many signs that day. They were all warning me to stay!

Nevertheless; ***I headed back to my addiction with eagerness of purpose.*** It was calling me from three hundred miles away and I could hear the demon! Its voice was loud and its **"gravitational pull"** was more powerful than a giant sun! I was being guided back for a life changing reason; money, death, myself or jail. What would it be?

I hit the road alone; ready for whatever was ahead of me. No longer could I run! At eleven that night; my drug addicted body made it back to the bright lights and corrupted roads of Dallas. It was the 7th day of the month and the 7th day of the week!

I called Stacy and she met me at a bar called the **Slip-out Lounge.** She pulled her vehicle beside mine and I got in.

The Adventures Of A Drug Addict

Stacy brought along her drug dealing roommate whom she sponsored.

I gave him the money for the ten pills and promptly swallowed two. She wanted to go back to her house and record music in her studio and so did I; but her roommate wanted to go to a new place called the **"After-Life."** It was a dwelling similar to **"Heaven!"** The unknown was around the corner.

I did not want to go but the drug was now my master. *Harry* had called to tell me that he would not be in town until the next day. I gave in and decided to go with *Stacy*.

I parked my car at a local hotel and got in with *Stacy*. We did the twenty minutes worth of driving to the west side of town. Her SUV drove us into the congregation of the *"walking dead"* and we arrived at the **"After-Life."**

I went in without reservations. It had the same vibe as **"Heaven"** but something just wasn't right. I decided to have a sit down because I didn't want to socialize with the other zombies! *Stacy* was moving around to the various rooms of darkness and drug abuse. I remained still.

As I sat under the hypnotic trance of the drugs and alcohol; *a beautiful Latino woman* dressed in red approached and asked if she could sit beside me. **She wanted drugs;** but I wasn't selling that night. The lady started to pressure me with flirtatious behavior. It was a look in her eyes that I couldn't put a finger on.

She said that she just wanted to get out of this place and go to a house party. I told her about Stacy and her studio. The lady said she

The Adventures Of A Drug Addict

just needed to get a few pills before leaving.

After about thirty minutes of conversation and aggression on her part; I gave in and handed the girl two of the party pills that I had gotten from Stacy.

She put them into her mouth and washed the drugs down with orange juice. I had sold thousands of dollars' worth of drugs in **"*Heaven"*** over the last few months, but this was one night I did not want to be a dealer or a pimp. I just wanted to be!

The girl sat close to me for the next twenty minutes and we talked. She then said that she had to go to the restroom and would be right back. Fifteen passed by and she was not back. I got up to go and find the lady; so that we could leave.

As I made my way toward the front to begin my search; masked men, dressed in black and armed with shotguns charged through the front entrance. They all had bullet-proof vest on and were yelling obscenities.

One of the men put the barrel of his long gun into my stomach and said, **"*Get on the fucking couch!"*** My body was motionless because of the cold steel that I could feel through my shirt. ***He helped me by giving me a strong push with his loaded weapon.*** I fell and stayed in a state of confusion.

It was thirty of these people with guns and they were ***yelling, cursing and giving orders.*** The frightened patrons ran and yelled! I stayed still! I still had not figured out who these masked thugs were!

The man who ordered me on the couch and who still stood over me with the barrel of his shotgun less than four inches from my eyes; ordered me to the room reserved for dancing. He marched me into the center of the **"After-Life!"**

The men had wrestled all of the drug induced **"*zombie-beings*"** there. At this time I realized that I was part of a raid by the **"*Drug task force.*"** I still had a few of the party pills on me, but I was so high that I couldn't remember where they were!

I reached down for my shirt, but my efforts were demobilized by the man with the gun and his command to keep my hands up! ***It was then that I saw her. Everything made sense!***

Seven people came in with masks on, but dressed in regular clothing. I immediately recognized her red clothing. It was the beauty that had persistently convinced me to give her two of the pills. I said, **"DAMN"** inside of my head because I knew what was about to happen.

She pointed to me in a hurry! The man with the gun led me outside where *local news crews were stationed.* I was eventually joined by about thirteen other dealers, drug users and the owner.

I was patted down for weapons and drugs. He found the six remaining party pills in my front pocket. When he pulled them out; I said, **"*Damn*"** again! I was caught red handed. I lowered my head in disappointment!

The Adventures Of A Drug Addict

The cameras caught a glimpse of my face as I was loaded onto the bus for criminals and jolted to the county jail. It was the first time I had ever been arrested. I was booked and given pink slippers to walk around in. **The false sense of security that the drug provided had worn off and I was left with truth to deal with.**

I thought about my *Father's words* and him not wanting me to go back to the city. I thought about me not telling him that I was leaving; because I knew that I shouldn't have! My brother had tried to convince me to stay but I denied his request.

All of the many warnings that I had before this day passed across the memory of my soul. The police robbing me, the flying-lights, my heart-problem that sent me to the hospital and the homeless man whom I met at the beginning of a new year flashed before me. I saw the hand in the window that saved my son, Tatiana, her mother and the evil voice that I heard in the hospital.

The near fatal killing of the State Trooper, the kidnapping of Red, the experience with Machi and Ideb and the darkness I felt coming from them was much. I had stolen from people and been involved in a woman's efforts to be an enslaved prostitute; because I was her pimp.

The drug dealing and the manipulation that comes with the territory, and the people that I used for my own selfishness; I was guilty of it all.
I had become evil and out of control. The drugs had taken over my life and the memories of painful events kept me from seeking help. It all came over me at once!

As I sat in the holding cell with others who had lost a grip on life and love; ***I listened to two seventeen year old boys who had just killed an eight month old baby.*** They were trying to shoot up a rival kid, but instead killed a child who was in a nearby car with her mother.

A man with much jail history confessed to the young boys and told them, ***"You want be going home."*** I saw one of the terrified boys who had become a killer break down and start to cry. His victim's life ended but his new reality was just beginning!

I was in the ***"Belly of The Beast"*** for three days. Finally, I was bonded out. But it was not the end of my addiction to the drugs. It still wouldn't let me go free! They wanted my life!

The Adventures Of A Drug Addict

Chapter 42
PLEASE DO NOT KILL ME!

My secret was out of the bag. I could no longer hide my addiction or my criminal lifestyle! My family begged me to come home when I got out of jail, but the urge to continue my binge was stronger! I wasn't finish yet!

Four days had passed since I got out of lockup. I only had fifteen dollars and did not have a place to stay. The only thing that I could think about was getting high. I called one of my drug connections to buy a single pill.

His name was *Bantu* and he was a Floridian. **He was a black gangster with many facial piercings.** I met him two years earlier and had spent thousands of dollars during this time buying his various drugs; some to sell and others to use.

When I met Bantu he was driving around in a beat-up and old Lincoln. Now he was rolling throughout town in a One Hundred thousand dollar car. **He also had an armed thug as his driver.** His ego had swollen.

He and his two brothers operated several *"trap houses"* around town and were making serious money. He stayed high on the various drugs that he sold but we never had any problems between us. I had even sold his brother some of my custom jewelry.

Bantu met me in the alley behind a closed business plaza. He pulled his new black luxury vehicle about ten feet behind mine. I got out of my car and into his.

The smell of weed, cocaine and liquor filled the inside. I told Bantu that I only wanted a single pill and that I was four dollars short on the price. He looked at me and said, ***"People always trying to fuck me!"*** His aggressive words indicated that he was on it all; alcohol, drugs and whatever else.

I told him that I would understand if he didn't want to do the simple drug deal. After a few seconds of hesitation; he said, ***"Give me the fucking money nigga."*** I exchanged my cash for the single drug.

I said, ***"I appreciate it"*** and got out of his car. I took two steps and he got out of his. He called my name and I turned around. He said, ***"Why do you want to fuck me bro?"*** His next moved shocked me! He pulled out his **"9mm semi-automatic handgun"** and aimed it for my face. The man had his finger wrapped around the trigger and was ready to shoot. I did not have time to think; I could only react!

I said, ***"Bantu, I will give it back to you and you can keep the money."*** I quickly summarized my suffering and my current hard times. I also reminded him that I had spent thousands with him. After a minute of listening; he put the gun back into his pants. He got in the car and his driver sped off!

I took a deep breath and fell to my knees in relief. It took me almost an eternity to walk back to my car. What had just happened?

The Adventures Of A Drug Addict

He was ready to kill me over four dollars.

I drove off and headed to a bar to try and enjoy the effects of the drug. It was near closing time and I gathered up the loose coins in the ashtray and bought a beer to go along with the half-pint of whiskey I had in my trunk.

I went in and sat alone. An hour passed and it was time for final call. I bought a beer to take with me as I left. My zombie like body walked out of the door.

When I got outside; a woman stopped me in my tracks. She said, **"Look at you. You don't even know who or what you are!"** I asked her what she meant by her words.

She said, **"You're the walking dead and I can see through you."** The woman frowned upon me and debased my being with truth. I became overwhelmed with embarrassment and shame.

She then looked at me and said, **"When HE saves You from the fire; go to Amelia Earhart School in Dallas, speak to the kids and give them what HE has given You!"** She put her hand on my shoulder and said, **"Go home in the morning."** The lady didn't say any other words and would not entertain any of mine.

She walked to a waiting car and they drove off. I was left with more than just wonder. I began to contemplate. I was going to die if I did not leave this place soon!

The next morning the reality had set in and I fairly comprehended that something wanted me to survive and not to die.

I took my guilt, shame, embarrassment and pride back to a simpler life to await my legal fate. *I headed east to Louisiana; the land of cotton, racism and poverty.* But the battle to heal from addiction and all of the many sins it had brought upon me would take years to recover from!

The Adventures Of A Drug Addict

Chapter 43
THE BEGGAR
&
THE
LEVITATING ARTIST

It had been three months and I was working on getting off of the drugs. My move back to Louisiana had reduced my habit because of a lack of money and a steady supply of the **"Sustenance."** I was getting better, but I had not recovered!

I had to go back to the city and see my lawyer. He was working on a deal to help me avoid prison time. He also needed to be paid.

I had been charged with multiple counts of delivery, manufacturing, possession and distribution of a "CDS" or "Controlled Dangerous Substance." I was facing five years in some Texas prison. The stress of possible jail time was aging me.

I arrived in the office of my lawyer and handed him more money. He began to tell me of the deal that the police had approached him with. **I could work for them as a confidential informant!**

Without any consideration; I quickly denied that offer. I said, **"FUCK NO!"** I was left with incarceration or probation as the other two options, but the outcome wasn't certain. My fate would either be in a **Judge's hand or "GOD'S Mercy!"**

I stayed the night in the city and decided to go out. My destination was downtown. I wanted to take in the familiar vibe of my recent past.

As I was walking to a favorite hang-out; I was stopped by a man that I knew. He was the former **"Owner of Heaven"** and sometimes a politician who ran for mayor. He had plans on changing American culture by opening thousands of similar drug infested clubs in every state. According to him; he would change the world this way.

The eccentric guy invited me into his new club and offered me VIP treatment. I went inside and took advantage of his bar; since it was all on the house. I had three drinks and decided to go outside for a bit of fresh air.

The owner had also went back outside and was soliciting others to come inside. A crowd of about seven people stood in a circle and smoked. I walked into the outer-realms of the group.

I observed a man walk up to them. **His cloths said that he was homeless and his eyes were blood red.** He was holding a notebook and a piece of a pencil.

The homeless looking man began asking the people if he could draw a picture for them. He wanted to buy himself some food. When the **club owner** overheard the conversation; he **walked up to the artist and began to speak harsh words to him.** He then grabbed him by the worn out coat and pushed him to the ground.

The Adventures Of A Drug Addict

I walked up in defense of this aged artist who was only asking for coins in exchange for his work. I told the owner who had once let me come into his club and sell drugs that he was wrong. I helped the old artist up to his feet.

The entrepreneur with the warped ideas about culture told me to never come back to his establishment and went back inside. The group of people that were watching the event laughed at me and the man who claimed to be an artist. I shook my head at them in disgust and started to walk away from the commotion.

The artist stopped me and said, *"Thank you."* I pulled out three dollars from my pocket and gave it to him. He begged to draw a picture of me.

I said OK and he and I walked across the street to the nearby alley where my car waited. When we made it there he began his work! He said, *"Express your feelings with a pose and I will capture your inner-self. It will be better than a picture."* I thought about his words. *My mood was one of revolution, anger, hurt, confusion, distrust, insecurity, shame, guilt, self-hate and hopelessness!* I threw my middle finger out at the world and held it in position for about four seconds. The old artist turned his notebook upside down and began to scribble. He would look up at me every five to six seconds and then his eyes would fall back unto the paper like a bouncing ball. I said in my mind, *"The old man is drunk."*

He carried on his artistic endeavors! He carried on for four more minutes. He then said, **"I'm finish!"**

The one who did not look like an artist turned the paper around and unveiled a perfect portrait of me. It was drawn with the speed of lightning and it was done backwards. I said, **"WOW."**

The old artist with red eyes said that he wanted to show me something else. I told him that the stage was his. He quietly spoke the words, **"Look at my feet."**

I looked down and he had ascended three feet off of the ground. I passed my foot under the place where he had just been standing. There was nothing but air.

I backed up and lost my footing on the concrete due to shock. My body landed on the hood of my car. As I tried to gather myself; I watched him descend back to the ground!

I saw his feet reconnect with gravity and he was standing again! I said, **"How did you do that?"** The man began to speak words that held no validity to my drug addicted corpse.

He said, "You will use this picture for a book one day. It has been ordained and will be a testimony for the Spiritual work ahead of You. Indeed You are blessed because Our **"FATHER"** has chosen to save You from Yourself and the **"hell"** that You have created. Remember these words when the time is right!"

Just as he finished talking; another man who looked just as poor and homeless came up.

The Adventures Of A Drug Addict

He said, **"It is time to go."** I tried to stop the man and question him on his words and his ability to levitate off of the ground. He wouldn't entertain my doubt and just said,

"Remember!"

The two old guys walked away fast and by the time I got into my car and gave chase; they had disappeared into the streets. I was left with wonder; as to how that man did what he did! I passed my foot under his and nothing stopped its course.

The next morning I headed back to the country. I could not quit thinking about the man that I saw float off of the ground.

Was it real?

If it was an illusion; how did he do it and why did he choose me to show his magic? His words did not make sense either. I wasn't a writer! But he did give me hope when he said that I had been chosen to be saved! Maybe I would be alright. ***Only time would tell!***

Chapter 44
FOLLOW THE LIGHTS

It was **August 29** and I had went to party with my friend. The local club had closed at 2am and the two of us went on a quest for our *drugs of choice*. After two hours of exploration and coming up empty; we abandoned the shady mission. I went back home and was forced to deal with me!

My reality set in. I was facing five years in jail! My life had become defined by drugs, alcohol and criminality. I was lost and confused about living. **Death seemed to be the only way out for me!**

My *"Sins"* had reached up to Heaven and I had become evil. The look in my eyes told the story of a journey through *"Hell!"* Death seemed to be the only way out for me!

With nothing to lose; I *poured* more of the *strong spirit* into my cup. The thoughts of my past had begun to sadden me. I just wanted the pain to end. I was at a limit!

I looked at my watch and it was after four in the morning. Sleep was foreign to me. *I had not slept in ten years!* So, I was just pacing up and down the driveway smoking cigarettes and drinking poisons to avoid a reflecting mind. The sky had cleared up from what had been a stormy night.

The Adventures Of A Drug Addict

The stars began showing their glory. I put my gaze towards the east and listened to the sounds of the night. Nature was the only voice that I could hear.

I saw what looked to be a plane coming from the direction that my vision was aimed. It was flying my way, but it was too low to be an airplane. I couldn't hear any propulsion as it approached.

The movements imitated that of a butterfly and it was inaudible. It was only about forty feet above me as it passed over the house. I could see its **shadowy metallic color.**

It didn't have any openings for the release of energy or any windows. The craft had the shape of a **triangle** and it was **flying** so very slow; maybe only **7mph.**

My **sight became blind** as it passed directly over my head and suddenly stopped! The vision of that day is recalled in this book for all to feel and read. This information is real and true to those who seek a way out. The **"Path of the Spirit"** is the way out of addiction and the way out of pain!

If you can identify, seek understanding and find the spirit; then you can heal from any past; no matter how wrong. Let go of the ego. Let go of you. Let go of your past. Follow the *"Lights"* because they do lead to "HIM!"

4:22AM
Follow the Lights

A-mista: My Son, do you know where You are?

Addict: I'm either dead or in jail.
Who are you?
Where am I at?
Why is light radiating from you?

A-mista: My Son, *You are lost.*
You have forgotten who You are, why You are here, where You came from and the importance of Your life to the many You are to help.
Your **FATHER** and My **FATHER** has seen Your afflictions, suffered the pain with You and has all-ways looked upon You with compassion and mercy.
Your day of Revelations, spirit insight, truth and healing has descended upon You from the universe of Your last sojourn and **MERCY** will be shown to You for the Glory of the **GREAT SPIRIT** and the message of Hope and Love that You will carry to those who are in need, as You, Yourself are now in need of guidance.

The Adventures Of A Drug Addict

Addict: Am I facing trouble?

A-mista: No my Son.
You are facing *"The Choice!"*

Addict: Well, I am leaving this behind Sir.
How do I get out of here?

A-mista: I will show You the way.
What is the last thing You remember my Son?

Addict: I remember a beautiful triangular craft hovering over ahead and then a radiant *"Light of SUPREMACY."*
But then, I heard the most Powerful, yet Gentle VOICE say, *"Follow the lights!"*
"They lead to ME!"

The Adventures Of A Drug Addict

The Adventures Of A Drug Addict

The Adventures Of A Drug Addict

The Adventures Of A Drug Addict

www.ingramcontent.com/pod-product-compliance
Lightning Source LLC
Chambersburg PA
CBHW061943070426
42450CB00007BA/1037